D1474682

WITHDRAWN
UTSA LIBRARIES

WITHDRAWN
UTSA LIBRARIES

Miguel de Unamuno's Quest for Faith

Miguel de Unamuno's Quest for Faith

A Kierkegaardian Understanding
of Unamuno's Struggle to Believe

Jan E. Evans

Foreword by
Stephen T. Davis

☙PICKWICK *Publications* · Eugene, Oregon

Library
University of Texas
at San Antonio

MIGUEL DE UNAMUNO'S QUEST FOR FAITH
A Kierkegaardian Understanding of Unamuno's Struggle to Believe

Copyright © 2013 Jan E. Evans. All rights reserved. Except for brief quotations in critical publications or reviews, no part of this book may be reproduced in any manner without prior written permission from the publisher. Write: Permissions, Wipf and Stock Publishers, 199 W. 8th Ave., Suite 3, Eugene, OR 97401.

New Revised Standard Version Bible, copyright 1989, Division of Christian Education of the National Council of the Churches of Christ in the United States of America. Used by permission. All rights reserved.

Scripture quotations marked (NIV) are taken from the Holy Bible, New International-al Version®, NIV®. Copyright © 1973, 1978, 1984 by Biblica, Inc.™ Used by permission of Zondervan. All rights reserved worldwide.

Pickwick Publications
An Imprint of Wipf and Stock Publishers
199 W. 8th Ave., Suite 3
Eugene, OR 97401

www.wipfandstock.com

ISBN 13: 978-1-62032-106-5

Cataloguing-in-Publication data:

Evans, Jan E., 1949–

    Miguel de Unamuno's quest for faith : a Kierkegaardian understanding of Una-muno's struggle to believe / Jan E. Evans ; foreword by Stephen T. Davis.

    xx + 132 pp. ; 23 cm. Includes bibliographical references.

    ISBN 13: 978-1-62032-106-5

    1. Unamuno, Miguel de, 1864–1936. 2. Unamuno, Miguel de, 1864–1936—Religion. 3. Unamuno, Miguel de, 1864-1936 —Criticism and interpretation. 4. Kierkegaard, Søren, 1813–1855. I. Davis, Stephen T., 1940–. II. Title.

PQ6639.N3 E93 2013

Manufactured in the U.S.A.

Library
University of Texas
at San Antonio

To my children,
Kelley, Lise and Chaz

Contents

Foreword

Stephen T. Davis
Russell K. Pitzer Professor of Philosophy
Claremont McKenna College

I

OF ALL THE TWENTIETH-CENTURY philosophers whom we call Existential-ists, Miguel de Unamuno wears best, speaks most powerfully to us today.[1] This great Spanish thinker (1864–1936) was an extraordinarily gifted man of letters. He was a philosopher, linguist, poet, novelist, short story writer, essayist, playwright, professor, university administrator, and Spanish public intellectual. He had great intellectual integrity and moral courage.

His *magnum opus*, *The Tragic Sense of Life* (1913),[2] constitutes the summation of his philosophy. In that book, we encounter an author who was struggling with God, reason, doubt, faith, and immortality. These, indeed, were almost the only philosophical issues that Unamuno wanted to write about. Abstruse questions in metaphysics, epistemology, logic, or even ethical theory had little interest for him. He was heir to the rich Span-ish Roman Catholic religious and intellectual tradition, but he lived in ten-sion with it for virtually all of his adult life.[3] Two of his books were placed on the Index of Forbidden Books by the Spanish religious hierarchy, yet he was a deeply religious (and arguably even Christian) man.

Unamuno is not an easy philosopher to read. He loved paradoxes and even (at times) contradictions. Various interpreters have called him an athe-ist, a skeptic, a Protestant, a panentheist, a Catholic modernist, and a good

---

1. Well, possibly Camus is the one exception.

2. Miguel de Unamuno, *Tragic Sense of Life*, trans. J. E. Crawford Flitch (New York: Barnes & Noble, 2006).

3. See, for example, his *The Agony of Christianity*, trans. Kurt F. Reinhardt (New York: Frederick Ungar, 1960).

Catholic. Passages can be found in his writings that can be taken to support all of these interpretations. In the present book, Jan E. Evans does an incisive and thorough job of sorting through the Unamuno corpus and arriving at a definitive interpretation of his views. One great asset of Evans' work is the insight she gains by comparing Unamuno's works with the philosophers whom he admired most and considered his fellow travelers in the tragic sense of life. They would be Pascal, William James, and especially Kierkegaard.

II

My own love of Unamuno began in college when *The Tragic Sense of Life* was recommended to me by one of my professors. I did not (and do not) share many of Unamuno's religious doubts. But I was captivated by the eloquence of his prose (even in translation), the depth of his knowledge of philosophy, theology, and literature, his insistence that philosophy must be relevant to real life, and his obviously sincere interest in helping his reader ("the man of flesh and bone") by his philosophy. But two other points stand out as well: first, I felt that here was a man who genuinely understood human nature and the human situation. Second, and most of all, I was struck by the passion and intellectual integrity with which he approached issues of faith, doubt, and God.

Unamuno was deeply interested in, indeed almost obsessed by, the topic of personal immortality. Thus he tells us that "as a youth, and even as a child, I remained unmoved when shown the most moving pictures of hell, for even then nothing appeared to me quite so horrible as nothingness itself."[4] Indeed, he allowed as how he could not understand those folks who claimed not to be disquieted by the thought of their eventual annihilation.[5] Moreover, he believed that apart from immortality or resurrection, life here and now has no meaning.

But he was convinced that the only sensible basis for belief in life after death was God. And here we see the central problem of Unamuno's philosophy: reason, he believed, cannot show that God exists or that the soul is immortal. Unamuno was convinced that the classic "proofs" of the existence of God are all fallacious, and in any case that the "God" they try to prove is not the Christian God. The God that emerges from the proofs,

4. Unamuno, *Tragic Sense of Life*, 8; cf. also 39.
5. Ibid., 106.

he says, is "nothing but an idea of God, a dead thing."[6] He believed further that reason actually shows the impossibility of individual consciousnesses persisting after bodily death.[7] Unamuno's philosophy amounted to an unrelenting tug of war between reason's doubts about God and immortality and the heart's desire for God and for life beyond death.

We cannot miss an interesting comparison between Unamuno, the religious doubter, and today's atheists (as exemplified by the "New Atheists" such as Dawkins, Hitchens, Dennett, et al.). They dismiss religion as frivolous nonsense; Unamuno took it with utmost seriousness and struggled with it. I myself have often wondered why the New Atheists are not more *puzzled by* religion, at the very least puzzled by the question of why so many intelligent people are religious. Nor do they seriously study (or even mention!) today's most gifted defenders of religion. Unamuno had no problem sympathetically understanding the faith of Spain's simple Catholics (although he could not share their faith); the New Atheists just cannot understand why anybody but a fool would embrace religion.

But Unamuno strongly wanted to believe; he took comfort from the story of the worried father in the Gospel of Mark who said to Jesus, "I believe; help my unbelief!" (Mark 9:14–29). And Unamuno tried to conduct his life *as if God existed*, i.e., he wanted to live, as much as possible, as Christians are commanded to live, especially through love and suffering. Thus he wrote, "To believe in God is to long for His existence and, further, it is to act as if He existed; it is to live by this longing and to make it the inner spring of our action. This longing or hunger for divinity begets hope, hope begets faith, and faith and hope beget charity."[8]

And as Evans does (see her concluding chapter), I deeply appreciate the way that Unamuno tried to live as a Christian in the public sphere. I am thinking especially of his words and deeds on behalf of freedom of thought and freedom of religion, as well as his opposition to all forms of political authoritarianism. Such opinions, courageously expressed by Unamuno, cost him dearly. In my view, he succeeded in acting as if God existed.

6. Ibid., 141.
7. Ibid., 92.
8. Ibid., 163.

III

It might help to clarify Unamuno's religious stance if we were to imagine different levels of religious belief and unbelief. I will describe five of them.

1. Total skepticism;
2. Honest doubt with no desire to believe;
3. Honest doubt plus a sincere desire to believe;
4. Belief informed by reason and doubt;
5. Simple faith.

The first, total skepticism is the position represented by the New Atheists, as well as many others today. Religious belief is dismissed as irrational and religious practice is considered a pointless waste of time. The second is the location of many people whom I know; they respect religious folk, have no desire to ridicule them, but for various reasons are unable to believe and have no desire to do so. The third is, I think, the position of Unamuno and, I am sure, a few others whom I have known. Intellectual scruples prevent them from believing, but they find something deeply attractive in religion and have a kind of nostalgia for belief and the life of faith. Maybe, like Unamuno, they even try to live as much as possible "as if God existed." The fourth, so far as I know myself, would be my own stance. I am a Christian believer but I certainly experience doubt and, as a philosopher of religion, I am acutely aware of the problems and objections that religion faces, most notably the problem of evil. And the fifth is the location of Unamuno's famous figure, the *carbonero*, the coal delivery man. Presumably Unamuno had in mind people of little education and maybe intelligence; the *carbonero* believes exactly what Holy Mother Church says, without doubt, scruple, or question.

Those, like me, who admire Unamuno might be tempted at this point to ask: of these five, which stances are religiously sufficient? Specifically, does Unamuno's position of honest doubt with a sincere desire to believe pass muster? But these questions are vague to the point of incoherence: sufficient for what? We might say: *sufficient to be acceptable to God*. That is, can a person who honestly doubts, sincerely wants to believe, and tries to live christianly inherit the kingdom of God? But of course that question is a non-starter. It is not given to human beings to know who will be part of the blessed and who part of the reprobate. That is up to God. Well, then we might say: *sufficient to be a Christian*. But then what is a Christian? There appear to be about as many ways of understanding the word "Christian" as there are people who ask the question. Think of the different answers that might be given by Fundamentalists, Pentecostals, Evangelicals, conservative Catholics, progressive Catholics, Eastern Orthodox believers, or members of mainstream Protestant denominations.

Moreover, even if we could find a satisfactorily precise question, answers to our sufficiency question would vary greatly depending on one's point of view. Obviously, pre-Vatican II Spanish Catholics of the early 1900s would be inclined toward a very different sort of answer than contemporary Catholics. This is not even to mention thousands of other possible views, including my own as an early twenty-first century Presbyterian. Despite my deep religious and philosophical respect for Unamuno, I can give no definite answer, even as a private opinion, on the question of whether Unamuno's religious stance passes muster. There is no clear question in the neighborhood and, even if there were, I do not know the mind of God.

Why then have I bothered to raise this point? Because it seems to me that *this is Unamuno's deepest issue*. Indeed, it is his most anguished worry. I am not aware of anywhere in his writings (much of which I have not read) where he asks the precise question whether he has done enough to merit or inherit eternal life. Nevertheless, I believe that this is his own most worrying question. And, finding no answer, he describes his position as tragic.

IV

As noted, Unamuno was convinced that life has no meaning apart from immortality, and that the hunger for life after death is the basis of all philosophy. Indeed, he held that if our individual consciousnesses do not survive death, "then is our labored human lineage no more than a fateful procession of ghosts, going from nothingness to nothingness and humanitarianism the most inhuman thing that is known."[9]

Accordingly, it might be interesting to ask what is so frightening about death. Why do people fear death? Why did Unamuno shrink from it? It appears that there are lots of reasons to fear death:

- Fear of dying painfully;
- Fear of hell or of some kind of painful existence in the afterlife;

9. Ibid., 38. Flitch's translation of this passage is problematic. The translation of the Spanish quoted here is from Jan Evans.

- Fear of the unknown (we have no clear idea of the afterlife);

- Fear of absolute solitude, isolation from others (if we could all hold hands and leap together into the void, perhaps death would not be so frightening);

- Fear of separation from my loved ones;

- Fear about the earthly fate of my loved ones after I die;

- Fear that my hopes, goals, and aspirations will be unfulfilled;

- Fear of being forgotten;

- Fear of non-being, of my total annihilation as a person.

Naturally, different people will rank these fears differently. But it is perfectly clear that it is the last fear listed that most deeply bothered Unamuno. He knew that Christianity teaches the general resurrection—that we will be bodily raised in the afterlife to be in the presence of Christ. But his doubts prevented him from rationally embracing the doctrine.

Yet Unamuno was convinced that out of the tragic sense of life—the despair and pain that unfulfilled religious longing entails—emerges hero-ics deeds, hope, and love. Thus he wants his reader to see "how out of this abyss of despair hope may arise, and how this critical position may be the well-spring of human, profoundly human, action and effort, and of solidar-ity and even of progress. He will see its pragmatic justification."[10] Reason separates us from God, Unamuno held, but we come to God by way of love and suffering. The knowledge of God, which is not rational, proceeds from the love of God.[11]

And there is even a kind of belief here. Unamuno's novella, *Saint Manuel Bueno, Martyr*, is clearly in part an *apologia* for Unamuno's own religious stance. It is the story of a saintly but unbelieving Spanish country priest who conceals his skepticism about God and the afterlife from all but two of the villagers. One of them is Ángela Carballino, the imagined nar-rator of Unamuno's tale, and the other is her brother Lázaro, who shares Father Manuel's unbelief. Some time after the death of both Father Manuel and Lázaro, Ángela writes, "Now, as I write this memoir, this confession of my experience with saintliness, with a saint, I am of the opinion that Don Manuel the Good, my Don Manuel, and my brother, too, died, believing they did not believe, but that, without believing in their belief, they actually

10. Ibid., 113–14.

11. Ibid., 148.

believed, in active, resigned desolation."[12] Or, as Unamuno says elsewhere, "faith continues to live on doubt."[13]

V

There are very many things that I deeply appreciate in Unamuno's philosophy. I will mention two such points.

First, his insistence that philosophy must be relevant to real life is one that I resonate with. Philosophy begins, and in my view must end, as an attempt to answer real questions asked by real people. This of course includes the questions that Unamuno asked, like, "Does God exist?" and "Will I live on after my death?" But it also includes such questions as, "How do I know what is morally right and morally wrong?" "What is the best form of government?" "Are human beings free in their decisions and actions?" "Are human beings physical bodies and nothing else?" "What is knowledge and how does it differ from other cognitive states?" and hundreds of others. Thus Unamuno wrote, "Philosophy is a product of the humanity of each philosopher, and each philosopher is a man of flesh and bone who addresses himself to other men of flesh and bone like himself. And, let him do what he will, he philosophizes not with the reason only, but with the will, with the feelings, with the flesh and with the bones, with the whole soul and the whole body. It is the man that philosophizes."[14]

Second, I agree that doubt is an important component of a mature faith. People who are raised in religious families and cultures sometimes go through a time of religious crisis, often during their teen-age years. Usually the problem is religious doubt. Some, of course, give up religion permanently. But others, largely by working with their doubts, emerge with a stronger faith, a faith that is no longer their parents' faith but is now uniquely theirs. Doubts are, or at least can be, good things. Although Unamuno was quite prepared to doubt reason, it worries me that it never seemed to occur to him to doubt his doubts.

But the paradox for me is that I am greatly attracted to Unamuno at the same time that I am repelled. I do not see reason as the enemy of faith; I do

12. Miguel de Unamuno, *Ficciones: Four Stories and a Play*, trans. Anthony Kerrigan, Selected Works of Miguel de Unamuno 7 (Princeton: Princeton University Press, 1976) 176–77.

13. Unamuno, *Agony of Christianity*, 44.

14. Unamuno, *Tragic Sense of Life*, 25.

not hold that faith in God and the resurrection is irrational; I do not accept the idea that the classical scholastic picture of God is self-contradictory; and I do not agree that the "God" that emerges from the theistic proofs is only an idea of God.

If Unamuno were alive today, he would be 148 years old. It is absurd to imagine him living that long and I suppose it is equally absurd to wonder how a human being who lived in one place and time would react to events occurring at another place and time. Despite the absurdity, I cannot help wondering how Unamuno would react if he knew of the revival of philosophy of religion and even of Christian philosophy among both Catholics and Protestants that began in the late 1970's and continues through today.

It is perfectly possible that he would be horrified by this movement. (Some people today react in such a way.) But I just wonder whether his religious doubts might have been assuaged at least to a certain extent if he were able to reads works of people like Alvin Plantinga, John Hick, Richard Swinburne, William Alston, Eleonore Stump, and a host of others. Obviously, there is no answer to such a question.

Be that as it may, I commend *Miguel de Unamuno's Quest for Faith* to the scholarly world. The book is clearly written, careful in its argumentation, and wonderfully perceptive. One of Evans' insights in chapter 5 caused me to see Unamuno in a new way. She claims—and I accept the point—that Unamuno was unhappy with God because God remains hidden, especially from reason. He was offended that the only avenue toward knowledge of God that God leaves open is revelation, which he could not accept.

Miguel de Unamuno, one of the great geniuses of twentieth century philosophy and Spanish literature, comes alive for us in this book. My fervent hope is that *Miguel de Unamuno's Quest for Faith* convinces the scholarly and philosophical world to start reading Unamuno again.

Acknowledgments

I AM ACUTELY AWARE that without the help and support of many this book would never have come to light. The initial work on this project was done during a research leave made possible by Baylor University. That leave was taken at Calvin College in Grand Rapids, Michigan where I had previously taught. Calvin welcomed me back as a visiting scholar and gave me access to their excellent library and work space. Most importantly, various members of the Spanish Department there talked through many of the ideas presented here with me. Chief among those was Cynthia Slagter who listened patiently, asked important questions and contributed much to the book's progress.

Once back in Texas, colleagues in Baylor's Division of Spanish and Portuguese provided help in reading chapters in their various states. I want to especially thank Michael Thomas, Frieda Blackwell and Paul Larson who allowed me to dominate many lunchtime conversations with my own questions and concerns about my project and whose wise counsel I needed throughout. The chair of the Department of Modern Foreign Languages, Heidi Bostic, has been enormously supportive of me, helping me find a workable balance between teaching, administrative and scholarly duties. I am grateful to Karl Aho for his genuine interest in the text and his careful work on the index.

I am especially indebted to Stephen Davis who agreed to write the thoughtful Foreword for this book. Davis is one of the few philosophers I know who has a genuine interest and appreciation for Miguel de Unamuno, an interest that stemmed, at least in part, from his association with John A. Mackay, the President of Princeton Theological Seminary (1936–1960), who had actually met and corresponded with Unamuno.

I am grateful to the following journals for permission to use in revised form material that originally appeared in these forms: "Miguel de

Acknowledgments

Unamuno's Reception and Use of the Kierkegaardian Claim that 'Truth is Subjectivity,'" published in *Revista Portuguesa de Filosofía*; "La metáfora de la llaga en Søren Kierkegaard y Miguel de Unamuno: La importancia del sufrimiento en la existencia auténtica," published in *Cuadernos de la Cátedra Miguel de Unamuno*; "Does Miguel de Unamuno's Doubt Keep Him from Faith? Some Considerations with Glances to Pascal and Kierkegaard," published in *Christian Scholar's Review*; "The Metaphor of the River in Unamuno's *El Cristo de Velázquez*: Subversive Text or Devotional Reading?" published in *Romance Notes*; "Unamuno's Passion for Immortality: Narcissism or Foundation for Religious Belief?" published in *Journal of Christianity and Foreign Languages*; and "Unamuno's Faith and Kierkegaard's Religiousness A: Making Sense of the Struggle," published in *Hispanófila*.

Last, but most certainly not least, I want to thank my husband, Stephen, for his help throughout the years of the making of this book. Not only do I depend on his extensive work on Søren Kierkegaard, I am grateful for his concern for the issue of Unamuno's faith, for his willingness to discuss the underlying problems with me, for his gentle feedback on the text, and for his constant love and encouragement.

Jan E. Evans
Baylor University, 2013

Abbreviations

PARENTHETICAL REFERENCES IN THE text to Unamuno's works are by volume and page number in the *Obras Completas* edited by Manuel García Blanco and published by Escelicer , Vols. 1–9, Madrid: 1966–1971. Translations of all Spanish quotations in the text are mine.

The following abbreviations occur in parenthetical references to works by Søren Kierkegaard.

CUP   *Concluding Unscientific Postscript to 'Philosophical Fragments'.* 2 vols. Ed. and trans. Howard V. Hong and Edna H. Hong. Princeton: Princeton University Press, 1992.

EO   *Either/Or.* 2 vols. Ed. and trans. Howard V. Hong and Edna H. Hong. Princeton: Princeton University Press., 1987.

EUD   *Eighteen Upbuilding Discourses.* Ed. and trans. Howard V. Hong and Edna H. Hong. Princeton, Princeton University Press, 1990.

FT   *Fear and Trembling* and *Repetition.* Ed. and trans. Howard V. Hong and Edna H. Hong. Princeton: Princeton University Press, 1983.

JP   *Søren Kierkegaard's Journals and Papers.* Ed. and trans. Howard V. Hong and Edna H. Hong, assisted by Gregor Malantschuk. Bloominton: Indiana University Press, (Vol. 1) 1967, (Vol. 2) 1970, (Vols. 3–4) 1975, (Vols. 5–7) 1978.

PF   *Philosophical Fragments* and *Johannes Climacus.* Ed. and trans. Howard V. Hong and Edna H. Hong. Princeton: Princeton University Press, 1985.

PV   *The Point of View for My Work as an Author.* Ed. and trans. Howard V. Hong and Edna H. Hong. Princeton: Princeton University Press, 1998.

Abbreviations

SUD   *The Sickness Unto Death.* Ed. and trans. Howard V. Hong and Edna H. Hong. Princeton: Princeton University Press, 1980.

UDVS   *Upbuilding Discourses in Various Spirits.* Ed. and trans. Howard V. Hong and Edna H. Hong. Princeton: Princeton University Press, 1993.

WL   *Works of Love.* Ed. and trans. Howard V. Hong and Edna H. Hong. Princeton: Princeton University Press, 1995.

1

Introduction

A Map for the Journey

MIGUEL DE UNAMUNO (1864–1936), Spain's most distinguished man of letters during the twentieth century, published in every possible genre—drama, poetry, the philosophical essay, the short story and the novel. Some readers of Spanish literature know him as a leader of the Generation of 1898, the group of writers who sought to redefine Spanish national identity after "El Desastre," the loss in the war with the United States in 1898. Philosophers will know him for his major philosophical work *Del sentimiento trágico de la vida* (*The Tragic Sense of Life*). Others know him best for his short novel *San Manuel Bueno, mártir (Saint Manuel the Good, Martyr)*, his story about an unbelieving priest whom the Church wanted to canonize.

This book examines the life and work of Unamuno through the lens of his faith. Because of the polemical nature of the Unamunian corpus and its breadth, there has been a substantial amount written on the faith of Miguel de Unamuno in Spanish and in English, though to my knowledge no entire book devoted to the topic in English. Those Hispanists who have access to the extensive bibliography on faith and Unamuno in Spanish will not find an exhaustive summary of that material here, but what they will find is a fresh look at some of the most vexing problems in Unamuno's understanding of faith. Those readers of English who are not familiar with Unamuno will find a clear exposition of the most important themes in Unamuno along with a framework through which one can profitably begin to read the primary works. No one book can encompass all that has been written about

Unamuno and faith, but I trust that both specialists and beginning readers will find in these pages helpful insights to enhance the reading of Unamuno and motivation to read more.

My aim in this work is to describe Unamuno's religious convictions in a sympathetic yet not uncritical manner. I will try to illuminate his faith with comparisons to thinkers Unamuno himself read, appreciated and appropriated, particularly Søren Kierkegaard (1813–1855), Blaise Pascal (1623–1662), and William James (1842–1910). Genuine religious beliefs are not just grist for unending debate; what one believes, if it is to be valid, must affect how one lives. This stance is Unamunian to the core, as we will see in chapter 3 as I discuss the nature of truth from Unamuno's perspective. I shall therefore begin with how life events affected the faith of Unamuno, but the book will end with an account of how Unamuno's faith shaped his life and his legacy.

Unamuno's religious convictions have proven difficult to pin down. Various critics have attempted to situate the Spanish philosopher within widely differing recognized religious traditions: Unamuno has been seen as a Catholic, a modern Erasmus, a Lutheran, a Protestant Liberal, a Krausist and a panentheist. Chief among the defenders of Unamuno as a Catholic is Julián Marías who sees in Unamuno's life a constant working out of the New Testament which Unamuno knew intimately.[1] Unamuno was called a modern Erasmus by the antagonistic government in Salamanca after the fateful day, October 12, 1936, in which he dared to oppose Franco's General Millán Astray in the Paraninfo of the University.[2] In an early article, Nemesio González Caminero lays the blame for Unamuno's loss of his Catholic faith and his "initiation" into the Lutheran faith at the feet of Kant.[3] Nelson Orringer has ably demonstrated the influence of Protestant liberal theologians like Ritschl and Harnack on Unamuno's thought, which Michael Gómez further illuminates in his study of religious modernism in Unamuno and Nietzsche.[4] In "The God of Unamuno," Armand Baker has a detailed exploration of Unamuno as a Krausist and panentheist, someone who believes that all life and nature are identical with God but who also believes that God is more than our understanding of life and nature. In

---

1. Marías, *Unamuno*, 144–45.
2. Lapuente, "Unamuno y la iglesia católica," 29.
3. González Caminero, "Las dos etapas católicas," 227.
4. Orringer, *Unamuno y los protestantes liberales.*

my view, none of these labels fits Unamuno very well, and I believe that he would have rejected all of them.

Some critics have even called Unamuno an atheist. The most strident of those is Antonio Sánchez Barbudo. In *Estudios sobre Unamuno y Machado* he says, "Unamuno era en verdad un ateo, pero tan anheloso de Dios, de eternidad, por un lado, y tan farsante y ansioso de fama, por otro; tan desesperado a veces y tan retórico otras muchas; y sobre todo, tan avisado, tan cuidadoso de ocultar su verdadero problema, esto es, su verdadera falta de fe."[5] ("Unamuno was in truth an atheist, but so desirous of God, of eternity on the one hand, and so anxious of fame making that a farce on the other, so desperate at times and so rhetorical many other times; and above all, so judicious and so careful to hide his real problem, that is, his true lack of faith.") Other commentators like Carlos Blanco Aguinaga in *El Unamuno contemplativo* find Sánchez Barbudo's judgments harsh and inaccurate because they do not take into consideration the whole of Unamuno's work.[6]

In January of 1957 the Catholic Church made its judgment official when it included two of Unamuno's works, *Del sentimiento trágico de la vida*, (*The Tragic Sense of Life*), and *La agonía del cristianismo*, (*The Agony of Christianity*), on its then extant Index of Forbidden Books. But already in 1903 Unamuno was condemned by the bishop of Salamanca, Fray Tomás de la Cámara, early in his career at the University of Salamaca,[7] and the same ecclesial office prohibited the reading of his *Del sentimiento trágico de la vida* in 1942.[8]

The heterodox nature of the Unamuno corpus gives rise to all of these theories. Much as one can give proof texts from the Bible to substantiate contradictory claims, some critics have gone to the works of Unamuno and have found passages to further their own agendas. Unamuno himself gives plenty of fodder for such critics because of his own penchant for contradiction; he does not want to be confined or limited by any school of thought. The purpose of this study is not to try out one more religious label on Unamuno but rather to appreciate the fullness of Unamuno's faith for what it is without shying away from saying what it is not.

I will speak about Unamuno's faith rather than Unamuno's religion. Whenever Unamuno takes up the topic of religion he gets combative, as in

5. Sánchez Barbudo, *Estudios sobre Unamuno y Machado*, 281.

6. Blanco Aguinaga, *El Unamuno contemplativo*, 290.

7. Lapuente, "Unamuno y la iglesia católica," 28.

8. Nozick, *Unamuno: The Agony of Belief*, 18.

his famous essay, "Mi religión." There he accuses those who would want to know what his religion is of wanting only to be able to categorize him or dismiss him. Those who demand to know what his religion is seem unaffected by the deep, eternal concerns of the heart, as he says, "se apartan de las grandes y eternas inquietudes del corazón" (3:261). ("They withdraw from the grand and eternal restlessness of the heart.") By contrast, Unamuno's essay, "La fe," ("Faith,") is a treatise that is full of passion and life rather than ridicule and defensiveness. There he says that faith is sincerity, tolerance and mercy (1:970).

I begin in chapter 2 with a narrative of what is known about the spiritually formative events of Unamuno's life, woven together with three of his works that are specifically aimed at questions of religious belief. *Diario íntimo* (*Inimate Diary*), *El Cristo de Velázquez* (*The Christ of Velázquez*), and *Agonía del cristianismo* (*The Agony of Christianity*) chronologically mark different moments in Unamuno's spiritual journey, but they address many of the same concerns. While some scholars carefully compartmentalize Unamuno's spiritual journey into specific periods of leaving his childhood faith, his embrace of Liberal Protestantism and his return to what he called "popular Spanish Catholicism," my emphasis is on the continuity of the critical questions with which Unamuno wrestled.

In chapter 3 I explore Unamuno's foundational notion of truth and the need for truth to have existential relevance. Here I begin the contrasts with Søren Kierkegaard, and it is right to pause a moment to justify the extensive use of Kierkegaardian thought in this book on Unamuno's faith. It is well known that Unamuno discovered Kierkegaard through reading criticism on Ibsen and that he purchased the first edition of Kierkegaard's *Samlede Værker* (*Collected Works*), when it was published from 1901 to 1906. The pages of almost all of the fourteen volumes are marked by Unamuno, both with glosses on the Danish in Spanish and German and also with marginal notations indicating passages of particular interest. But Unamuno was widely read in theology and philosophy. Why take Kierkegaard, and (I should add) Pascal, as interlocutors here? The major reason is the honor Unamuno bestowed on the two philosophers and the seriousness with which he took their thought.

In the first chapter of *Del sentimiento trágico de la vida* Unamuno names Kierkegaard as one of the men who possesses the tragic sense of life. Kierkegaard is a man who is "cargado de sabiduría más bien que de ciencia," ("burdened with wisdom rather than knowledge,") one who understands that if philosophy is to matter, it has to be lived (7:120). In *Agonía del cristianismo* Unamuno so identifies with both Pascal and Kierkegaard that he says, "Pero éste he sido yo! Y he revivido con Pascal en su siglo en en su ámbito, y he revivido con Kierkegaard en Copenhague" (7:314). ("But I have been this person! And I have lived again with Pascal in his century and in his environment, and I have lived again with Kierkegaard in Copenhagen.") In the passage in which this quote appears Unamuno is talking about how he reads an author, saying that he doesn't read to argue with a writer but rather attempts to become that person, that soul, in order to glean the truth from him. There is much in the Kierkegaardian and Pascalian soul with which Unamuno resonates, but I will show that Unamuno mainly appropriates the agonic, conflicted elements of their writings and little of their attempts to resolve that conflict. So it is appropriate to critique Unanuno's views through a wider reading of these writers whom he valued.

I explore the concept of "lived truth" in the third chapter through the Kierkegaardian claim that "truth is subjectivity." Unamuno begins his most philosophical work with the declaration that a philosopher must first be a man for whom the truth that he seeks affects the way in which he lives. A study of *Concluding Unscientific Postscript* and Unamuno's response to it allows us to understand the nature of lived truth. Here we see that propositional truth is always an approximation, that one never fully arrives at ultimate truth. Because of that, truth claims are always held modestly and with an awareness of their uncertainty. Truth only becomes truth as it is acted on in passion and becomes embodied in a person's life. All of the above are part of the Unamunian and Kierkegaardian soul, but there are significant differences in how each of the authors construes objective truth which will be outlined carefully.

Chapter 4 takes up the truth on which Unamuno would act passionately for his entire life after his spiritual crisis of 1897. That truth is the inevitability of death and the deeply felt need for there to be life after this one. Immortality and Unamuno's multi-faceted struggle with how one can attain it is the focus of this chapter. I will here draw again from *Diario íntimo* as Unamuno considers possible ways for one to live on after death. Even though it seems as if Unamuno's obsession with immortality is almost narcissistic at times, his passion will be seen as the impetus for the development of the Unamunian concept of *querer creer*, (wanting to believe), of the importance of the will to believe in the formation of belief. Although Unamuno rejects the normal proofs for God's existence and says many times that his own faith was destroyed by trying to rationalize God, he presents a compelling and richly intricate ground for belief in God, the only possible guarantor of our living after death. To justify a belief in the God who would be the guarantor of eternal life, Unamuno borrows from and builds on the philosophy of William James. Whether or not Unamuno ultimately believed in that God is still questionable because of Unamuno's insistence on the role of doubt in faith, which brings us to chapter 5.

In this chapter we take up the following questions as they are posed by Unamuno, Kierkegaard and Pascal. Is doubt a necessary part of faith? Are doubt and faith mutually exclusive? Are there dangers in claiming certainty for belief? Although a nuanced explanation of his view is necessary, Unamuno would say yes to all of these questions, and he believes that Kierkegaard and Pascal agree with him. The nature and the uses to which reason can be put are the central issues at stake in this discussion of doubt and faith. While I will argue that Kierkegaard and Pascal share much of Unamuno's view, it is ultimately Unamuno's view of reason that is the source of his inability to make the leap of faith that Kierkegaard and Pascal make. Kierkegaard and Pascal see that there are limits to human reason and this makes them approach the problem of the "hiddenness of God" very differently than does Unamuno. One can reasonably ask if Unamuno's stance of privileging doubt over faith keeps him from the more robust Christian faith of Kierkegaard and Pascal.

When doubt is applied equally to faith and to reason, the end result is a life of struggle. Unamuno does not back down from his embrace of a life of conflict and even goes so far as to use the metaphor of the "unhealed wound" to describe the life of longing to which he calls his reader. The unhealed wound is a metaphor that is found in Kierkegaard's *Concluding Unscientific Postscript* and one that I believe Unamuno seized on, believing that Kierkegaard's view of the necessity for suffering for authentic human existence was correct. Chapter 6 will show the origins of the metaphor of the unhealed wound in both authors and then will set out the similarities and the differences in the two authors' views of suffering. Our present culture avoids suffering through physical and mental therapies for every type of ailment. These two authors offer an important counter-discourse for our twenty-first century aversion of suffering, but the ultimate purposes of that suffering are very different in Unamuno and Kierkegaard, and those goals should be clear to anyone who would take up the possibility of seeing positive ends for suffering.

The comparison of Unamuno with Kierkegaard and Pascal leads to the conclusion that Unamuno cannot be considered to have the faith of an orthodox Christian. Nevertheless, there is much that a seeker of religious truth can find in Unamuno. Chapter 7 will offer an appreciation of the depth of Unamuno's faith using the category of Kierkegaard's Religiousness A, once again found in *Concluding Unscientific Postscript*. Religiousness A is one of the stages of existence that Kierkegaard believes must be traversed if one is to achieve authentic existence. It comes after the stages of the esthetic and the ethical and before Religiousness B, which is Christianity. Its requirements of resignation, suffering and guilt are very high, and Unamuno fulfills most of those requirements. Unamuno's faith is at once demanding and life encompassing. Most certainly, it has consequences for how one will live.

The final chapter will describe how Unamuno lived out his faith. It is only fitting that Unamuno be judged in this way. Unamuno claims that truth must be lived and his truth, his faith is *querer creer* (to want to believe). "Creer en Dios es anhelar que le haya y es, además, conducirse como si le hubiera; es vivir de ese anhelo y hacer de él nuestro íntimo resorte de acción. De este anhelo o hambre de divinidad surge la esperanza; de ésta la fe, y de la fe y la esperanza, la caridad" (7:219). ("To believe in God is to long for his existence and is, besides, to conduct oneself as though he existed; it is to live from this longing and make of it our intimate spring of action. From this longing and hunger for divinity rises hope, and from hope, faith and from faith and hope, love.") There are certainly practical, ethical and political consequences to Unamuno's faith. It is important to record the actions taken by this Spanish philosopher that affected the trajectory of Spanish history, actions that sprang from his faith and his longing for God to exist. Only then can one properly appreciate the strength and the validity of Unamuno's faith.

2

Miguel de Unamuno's Life and Spiritual Formation

HOWEVER HETERODOX AND COMPLEX Miguel de Unamuno's faith may be, it must be understood in the context of his life, and so this book begins with the story of how events in his life helped to shape his spiritual journey and ends with the story of how his faith affected his passions and his actions. The narrative of Unamuno's life is dramatic, and much would be lost in our understanding of the Unamuno corpus, both fiction and non-fiction, if we were to remain ignorant of his life.[1] At the same time, any attempt to explain the philosophical and theological basis for Unamuno's faith would be a vain exercise without acknowledging the consequences of his faith for how he lived. Unamuno would want it to be so. He would invite the reader to judge him by his actions because he says that truth is whatever is believed with one's heart and soul and to believe is to act in accordance with that belief (3:864).

The focus of this chapter is a chronological recounting of historic events in Unamuno's life along with an account of his writing about faith at critical moments of his life. Although I believe that Unamuno's faith commitments affected his fictional narratives, in order to say anything credible about what those faith commitments are one must look to the non-fictional

1. There are always risks in delving into an author's life and bringing his personal story to bear on his literary production. One should be careful with one's claims about how a particular event affected an author's writing. I take these concerns to be particularly important when one is dealing with fictional narrative where one needs to separate what Wayne Booth calls the "career author," from the "implied author," who may be "a dramatized narrator" or not and who further may be reliable or not. These distinctions are made in Booth, *Critical Understanding*, 269–70, and Booth, *Rhetoric of Fiction*, 149–65.

texts where the author addresses faith concerns directly. Throughout the telling of Unamuno's life story I will relate the events to as many of these non-fictional texts as possible within the space of these pages, but I will especially comment on *Diario íntimo* (*Intimate Diary*), written between 1897–1902, *El Cristo de Velázquez*, (*The Christ of Velázquez*), published in 1920, and *La agonía del cristianismo* (*The Agony of Christianity*) published in 1925, as they mark specific turning points in Unamuno's spiritual history.

The year 2012 marked the 75th anniversary of the death of Miguel de Unamuno and one might reasonably ask, how accurate are the historical records of Unamuno's life? Until 2009, the standard for biographical information on Unamuno was *Vida de Don Miguel* (*Life of Don Miguel*), by Emilio Salcedo with a prologue by Pedro Laín Entralgo, first written in the 1960's. Of course, there were those texts that are autobiographical in nature written by Unamuno, *Recuerdos de niñez y de mocedad* (*Memories of Childhood and Youth*), and his novel *Paz en la guerra* (*Peace in War*), that give insight into his childhood and his university years respectively. However, it is the monumental work of Collette and Jean-Claude Rabaté, French Hispanists, who have written the definitive story of the life of the Spanish philosopher in an 800 page volume entitled simply, *Miguel de Unamuno*. Publishing the book in December of 2009, the Rabatés have used wide and varied sources, most uniquely, the personal correspondence between Unamuno and his son, Fernando, to give the most complete view we have of his life to date. The image of Unamuno that emerges from its pages is that of the political Unamuno, a story that the authors believe has not been told adequately before. This view does not dwell on the man of faith whose story we are interested in here, but I am indebted to both of these sources as well as the biographical work of scholars Patrocinio Ríos Sánchez and Nelson Orringer for their help in telling this version of Unamuno's life story. In the following pages I sketch the historical events which affected his spiritual development. I will discuss some of the other authors that influenced his faith journey, but my narrative will be centered in what Unamuno himself said about religious faith over the decades.

Born in 1864 in Bilbao, young Miguel de Unamuno was brought up primarily by his mother and his grandmother, devout Catholics who were in the habit of daily mass and the practice of the sacraments of confession and communion. Unamuno's father, who at one point emigrated to Mexico in order to enhance his financial position, died when the young boy was six. There are two important things that the young Miguel inherited from his father, his library and his love for languages. In *Recuerdos* Unamuno recounts the story of his father entertaining a visitor from France in the sitting room where children were not normally invited. His father communicated with his guest in French. Young Miguel was amazed that the two men could understand each other in the same way that "we" understand each other, and he says that it was the beginning of his fascination with languages.

Unamuno reveals that his response to the rigors of religious devotion was typical of a child and not particularly edifying. Praying the rosary was "aquella molestia" ("that bother"). The repeated prayers, said as they knelt on hard benches were senseless to the young Miguel. The only way to get through them was to entertain himself with the varying sibilant sounds that he could make at the ends of words or other twists of pronunciation. Later, after reading that by repeating prayers one could earn indulgences, young Miguel and a cousin spent an afternoon shoring up years of indulgences for themselves (8:104).

Unamuno says that as a child he equated God and the devil with a night time monster "El Coco." As a child he feared the dark more than he feared death, because like all children he did not understand death. Nevertheless, he remembers the moment when death became real to him: a classmate died. For the young Miguel, heaven and hell were merely part of childish rhymes. As far as new experiences remembered, in *Recuerdos* Unamuno rates his first communion lower than going to the theater for the first time. He says he remembers little from his first communion, only that it was hyped a great deal and it left him cold. "Tanto le habla al niño de delicias y consuelos que no necesita porque no se halla desconsolado ni afligido" (8:128). ("They talk so much to a child about the delights and the comfort of which he has no need because he does not find himself to be disconsolate nor afflicted.")

It was in his father's library that the young Miguel was introduced to the great philosophers of the world—René Descartes (1596–1650), Immanuel Kant (1724–1804), and George Wilhelm Friedrich Hegel (1770–1831)—through the Spanish authors Jaime Balmes (1810–1848) and Juan Donoso (1809–1853). Unamuno says of that time in early adolescence, "Enamorábame de lo último que leía, estimando hoy verdadero lo que ayer absurdo; consumíame un ansia devoradora de esclarecer los eternos problemas; sentíame peloteando de unas ideas en otras, y este continuo vaivén, en vez de engendrar en mí un escepticismo desolar, me daba cada vez más fe en la inteligencia humana y más esperanza de alcanzar alguna vez un rayo de la Verdad" (8:144). ("I fell in love with whatever the last thing was that I read, believing true today what had seemed absurd yesterday. I was consumed with a voracious desire to clarify the eternal problems. I felt as though I were bandying about ideas, one against another, and this continual swinging from one point to another, instead of engendering in me a forlorn skepticism, gave me each time more faith in human intelligence and more hope in sometime obtaining a ray of Truth.")

During this formative time in his life Unamuno recalls with fondness the congregation with which he worshipped. He was integrated into it as a leader which brought him close to its director (8:146). He was particularly taken with a service called "las seisenas" which was held at dusk in a chapel full of shadows. He says that the space and the particular meditations that were read were fertile ground for his imagination, and pointedly, not for his reason. It was there that he dreamed about becoming a saint, but he says that dream was cut short by the frequent intervention of the image of a woman, described in all her womanly glory, which caused the dream of sainthood to fade quickly (8:147–48). It was the image of Concha de Lizárraga, his first and only love who would become his wife.

An episode that is reported by both Salcedo and the Rabatés, with sources from letters written to friends by Unamuno much later in life, is that as a child he felt a personal call to become a priest as he read his Bible and it opened by chance to, "Go and preach the Gospel to all the nations."[2] Unamuno says that many years later, after his relationship with Concha was well established, he remembered that first incident, and he purposed to confirm the call by opening his Bible at random again. This time he read from John 9:27, "I have told you already and you did not listen. Why do you want to hear it again?" Unamuno says of this event,"El recuerdo de aquellas palabras me ha seguido siempre."[3] ("The memory of those words have followed me always.")

Although Unamuno regularly criticizes the system of education in Spain in the *Recuerdos* and in many other places in his writings, he ends by saying of his years of bachillerato, "Salí enamorado del saber" (8:151). ("I left, in love with learning.") He happily went to Madrid to pursue the doctorate in 1880 at the tender age of sixteen full of great hope, though the year was also marked by the death of his grandmother. It was his grandmother's modest wealth that made it possible for Unamuno to go to Madrid and

2. Salcedo, *La vida de don Miguel*, 37, and Rabaté and Rabaté, *Unamuno*, 39–40.

3. Unamuno, "Carta a Ilundain," 48.

matriculate in the University. The Rabatés note that in 1877, three years before Unamuno started his university studies, illiteracy in the general population was 71 percent.[4] University education was for the privileged and for those who would lead the nation.

Unamuno's first university years were characterized by isolation and loneliness. He was very homesick for his home in Bilbao and he missed Concha. His lack of friends caused him to study all the more and he absorbed the reigning paradigms of the age. Although there were those of his professors who were still defending Catholic scholasticism, newer ideas were flowing into the university: Darwinism, positivism, and Krausism.[5] Between 1880 and 1884 he is said to have studied the European philosophy in vogue at the time, which included Kant, Hegel and Herbert Spencer (1820–1903). Unamuno did frequent the debates in the Ateneo and used its library, though much of the time feeling the outsider.[6]

As a response to his loneliness in his first year, Unamuno sought refuge in religious practices, going to mass regularly and taking communion monthly. But during his second year he began to seriously question Catholic dogma and speaks disparagingly of "la fe del carbonero," the unquestioning faith of the uneducated, personified in the coal delivery man. At particular issue was the belief in hell which Unamuno rejected. He later stated in *Diario íntimo*, "Por el infierno empecé a rebelarme contra la fe, lo primero que deseché de mí fue la fe en el infierno" (8:793). ("Through thinking about hell I began to rebel against faith; the first thing that I threw out was faith in hell.") Unamuno stopped going to mass. According to the Rabatés Unamuno regained a modicum of faith before leaving Madrid, though his understanding of God had been widened, as it was freed from traditional views of a jealous, punitive God to one that was more loving and accepting of all of his creatures.[7] Nevertheless, when he returned to Bilbao it was difficult to explain, much less to have his mother and Concha understand, the change in his religious views. Unamuno did not attend the ceremonies that would have conferred on him the doctorate, but rather petitioned for his degree to be conferred through the civil government of the province of

---

4. Rabaté and Rabaté, *Unamuno*, 54.

5. A particular sort of pantheism that was advocated by a German philosopher who came up with the term *panentheism* to describe how nature and all of human consciousness is a part of God, though God is more than just the collection of human consciousness.

6. Rabaté and Rabaté, *Unamuno*, 59.

7. Ibid., 62.

Vizcaya. The Rabatés speculate that his absence from the ceremony might have been due to the fact that, at that time, all conferees were required to swear that they believed in God, were Catholics, and upheld all of the dogmas of the Holy Roman Catholic Church.[8]

Unamuno returned to Bilbao and the house of his mother, with whom his relationship was very tense. He was unsuccessful in competing for various university posts and was reduced to teaching children wherever he could. The only light in this dark time of difficult living was Concha, the prospect of their marriage and their having as many children as possible. Concha was not formally educated, but Unamuno respected her intelligence and asked her to read drafts of his articles. She is said to have civilized Unamuno, teaching him social graces he sorely needed and bringing him out of his tendency to be a recluse. Most importantly, she encouraged Unamuno to try to recover the faith of his childhood, persuading him to reconnect with the spiritual advisor of his youth, Father Juan José de Lecanda, who was then located in Alcalá de Henares. Unamuno writes in one of his notebooks, "¿Tiene algo de extraño que yo después de haber guardado puercos en la piara positivista vuelva como el hijo pródigo a la casa de que salí ? . . . La felicidad consiste en gran parte en saber creer; esto me lo ha enseñado una mujer."[9] ("Doesn't it seem strange that I, after having kept the pigs in the swineherd of positivists, have returned like the prodigal son to the home from which I left? . . . Happiness consists in great part in knowing how to believe; this a woman has taught me.")

In January of 1891 Concha and Miguel were married, but they returned to the familial house in Bilbao, Unamuno having no means to obtain a home elsewhere. However, in May of the same year he was able to compete for and finally secure a post as a professor of Greek at the University of Salamanca where they moved and were able to make their first home. Unamuno was to have his desire to have children fulfilled quickly—Fernando, born in July of 1892, Pablo in January of 1894, and Raimundo in January of 1896. Sadly, Raimundo was stricken with meningitis which left him with hydrocephalus. At first there was some hope that he might be cured, but within a short time it was clear that would not be the case, though the boy might live for a long time with reduced mental capacities in a state of pain. Unamuno wrote to a friend, "Hasta hoy es pequeño el aumento de la cabeza . . . Usted sabe cuán escasas son las probabilidades de cura y como no es

---

8. Ibid., 67.

9. Unamuno, quoted in Rabaté and Rabaté, *Unamuno*, 106.

el peor resultado la muerte sino que ésta se dilata años que son años de imbecilidad e idiotismo para el pobre niño . . . Con esta desgracia hemos estado mi mujer y yo sin ganas para cosa alguna."[10] ("Until now the growing of the size of the head is small . . . You know how scarce the possibilities of a cure are and as the worst result is not death but rather that death lingers and there are years of imbecility and idiocy for the poor child . . . With this misfortune my wife and I have been without desire to do anything.") Both Salcedo and the Rabatés indicate that Unamuno felt somehow responsible for this terrible turn of events. Salcedo speculates that Unamuno felt that the illness was punishment for his pride.[11]

In these same first years as *catedrático* (tenured professor) at Salamanca, Unamuno declared himself a socialist and began to write for *La Lucha de Clases,* (Class Struggle). That in itself was cause for the citizens of Salamanca to question his suitability for teaching young minds, but Unamuno was not doctrinaire in his acceptance of Marxism and quickly fell out of favor with the editors of the journal. The pressures of writing and translating to add to his meager salary as a professor to support his family increased. With all of the strain of his university responsibilities, his family, and his reputation, Unamuno came to a point of near collapse. There are many accounts of what happened on the night of March 21 into the morning of March 22, 1897, but they all contain the following: Unamuno suffered the physical symptoms of a heart attack—heart palpitations and chest pain that extended to his arm—but the mental stress of facing death and the nothingness beyond produced equal anguish and pain. He sobbed, and he is said to have let out an incontrollable scream which frightened Concha, but she was able to embrace him and calm him with the strength of a mother and the words, "Hijo mío" ("My son"). In the wee hours of the morning Unamuno left the arms of his wife to go to the refuge of a Dominican convent to pray where he stayed for three days. The most immediate record of this life changing crisis is the letter which Unamuno wrote to the spiritual director of his youth, Juan José de Lecanda, written on March 22.

On March 23 Unamuno began his *Diario íntimo* with an entry about Raimundo, fragmented thoughts flowing from the stream of a tortured conscience. "¿Estará ciego? Experiencias. Indigestiones. Baños. Remordimientos ulteriores. La cabeza le crece . . . De noche me levanto a pasearle; besos más ahincados. Mis dos otros niños hacían mi orgullo; a la desgracia de éste se

10. Ibid., 133.

11. Salcedo, *La vida*, 89.

une una estúpida vanidad. ¡A luchar!" (8:775). ("Will he be blind? Experiences. Indigestions. Baths. Ulterior remorse. The head grows . . . At night I get up to walk with him; even more insistent kisses. My other two children became my pride; to the misfortune of this one is joined a stupid vanity. To struggle!") In the subsequent entries for the days immediately following this abrupt beginning, there are references to the child again, watching his development carefully and celebrating his every improvement. But what follows in the rest of the *Diario íntimo* is Unamuno's attempt over the next three years to recover his faith. An early entry says, "Con la razón buscaba un Dios racional, que iba desvaneciéndose por ser pura idea, y así paraba en el Dios Nada a que el panteísmo conduce, y en un puro fenomenismo, raíz de todo mi sentimiento de vacío. Y no sentía al Dios vivo, que habita en nosotros, y que se nos revela por actos de caridad y no por vanos conceptos de soberbia. Hasta que llamó a mi corazón, y me metió en angustias de muerte" (8:778). ("With reason I searched for a rational God who disappeared by being pure idea, and thus God ended up as the Nothingness to which pantheism takes you, and in a pure phenomenalism, root of my feeling of emptiness. I did not feel God alive, God who inhabits us and who is revealed to us through acts of charity and not by vain concepts of pride. Until he called to my heart and he put me in anguish of death.")

Within the first pages of the *Diario* Unamuno recognizes his own pride as a stumbling block to faith. "Nunca he podido ser un sectario, siempre he combatido todo dogmatismo, alegando libertad, pero en realidad por soberbia, por no formar en fila ni reconocer superior ni disciplinarme," (8:780). ("I have never been able to be a sectarian; I have always fought against dogmatism, allegedly for the sake of freedom, but in reality it was because of pride so that I wouldn't have to fall in line or recognize something else as superior or discipline myself.") He asks for humility, even in his use of reason. Certainly at the beginning there is an enormous sense of the need for repentance and contrition. "Lo que lloré al romper la crisis fueron lágrimas de angustia, no de arrepentimiento. Y éstas son las que lavan; aquéllas irritan y excitan" (8:783). ("What I cried at the outbreak of the crisis were tears of anguish, not of repentance. The latter are those that cleanse; the former are those that irritate and excite.") More than once he comments on his inability to cry.

In time, there are entries that reflect Unamuno's questioning of his own "conversion." He does not want it to be for show, for what may be made of it among his readers. The fundamental theme with which Unamuno would struggle for the rest of his life and the rest of his corpus is presented early: "Sólo se comprende la vida a la luz de la muerte" (8:786). ("One only comprehends life in the light of death.") Since the document covers essentially the time between the initial crisis, March of 1897, and the two years thereafter, (the last entry is January of 1902 but there is little between May of 1899 and that date) what is recorded are deep swings in the spiritual state of the author. There are periods of great dryness, of Unamuno's crying out as he feels the silence of God. Throughout there is the juxtaposition of faith and reason which would also characterize Unamuno's work for the next decades. In all, Unamuno seems to be fighting the statement that he makes, "Qué persona ilustrada y nutrida de ciencia tiene fe?" (8:810). ("What enlighted person, nurtured by science has faith?") He sees that intellectualism is a disease from which he wants to be cured, but at the same time he cares what his intellectual peers are saying about his "change." He is consumed by doubt, and he asks in prayer to be given certainty in faith. "Dame, Señor, absoluta fe y ella será la prueba de sí misma y de su verdad," (8:799). ("Give me, Lord, absolute faith and it will be the proof of itself and of your truth.") But the doubts return, over and over again.

Is there any resolution to all of the questions, any hope in all of the torment? There are accounts about the immediate religious retreat that Unamuno did with his spiritual director in Alcalá de Henares during holy week of 1897, just after the March crisis. In the entry for Easter Unamuno records, "No he resucitado todavía a la comunión de los fieles" (8:798). ("I have not been resurrected to the communion of the faithful yet.") However, in the following months there emerges the outline of the ways in which Unamuno would work out his own salvation. Reason would never prove God's existence. Only the existence of love would point in his direction. "¡Augusto misterio el del amor! La existencia del amor es lo que prueba la existencia del Dios Padre. El amor, no un lazo interesado ni fundado en provecho, sino el amor, el puro deleite de sentirse juntos, de sentirnos hermanos" (8:800). ("Wonderful mystery, that of love! The existence of love is what proves the existence of God the Father. Love, not the selfish bond founded on advantage, but love, the pure joy of feeling ourselves together, of feeling ourselves to be brothers.")

Unamuno describes two possible roads to faith: prayer and works of charity. Prayer is a mystery that must be experienced without scrutinizing it or quibbling about it. He has a strong sense that the practices of faith, particularly works of love towards one's neighbor, will bring one to faith. Act as though you believe, and you will. "Hay que ir por las obras a la fe para que la fe vivifique y justifique a las obras. Obra como si creyeras y acabarás creyendo para obrar" (8:854). ("One must go by works to faith so that faith may give life and justify the works. Work as though you believe and you will end up believing in order to act.")

Most importantly, it is here in the *Diario íntimo* that Unamuno articulates his doctrine of *querer creer* (to want to believe). Much will be said about this in the pages to come, but for now it should be noted that Unamuno defines faith as wanting to believe soon after the March, 1897 crisis. "Al encontrarme vuelto al hogar cristiano heme hallado con una fe que más que en creer ha consistido en querer creer" (8:797). ("When I found myself back in my Christian home, I found myself with a faith that consisted more in wanting to believe than with belief.") Later he claims faith through wanting to believe for himself. "Es ya gracia el deseo de creer, que nos hace merecer la gracia de orar y con la oración logramos la gracia de creer. Me complazco en creerlo así y al creerlo así, ¿no es, Señor, que creo ya en Ti?" (8:837). ("The desire to believe is a grace which makes us merit the grace to pray, and with prayer we achieve the grace to believe. I am comforted to believe this way, 'Do I not already believe in you, Lord?'") So Unamuno seems settled in his acceptance of his own sense of faith, of wanting to believe, though the place of doubt in the maintaining of that faith is affirmed to the last pages of the *Diario* where he says, "¿Por qué dudamos? ¿Por qué no reconocemos a Jesús verdadero hijo de Dios? Entonces pasaríamos sobre el tiempo, sin hundirnos en él" (8:879). ("Why do we doubt? Why do we not recognize Jesus as the true son of God? Because we would pass through time without sinking into him.") So within the *Diario íntimo* we see themes that are present and are more fully developed in later works:1) the impossibility of rationally knowing that God exists, 2) the importance of love and acts of charity for giving meaning to life, 3) the fact that faith gives life and reason leads to pride and paralysis, 4) that doubt is essential to deepen faith and 5) that wanting to believe is itself enough for faith.

I agree with respected scholar Patrocinio Ríos Sánchez, who says that Unamuno's spiritual biography can be divided into three stages.[12] The first, in his view, includes Unamuno's childhood faith, his tendency toward atheism in his university years and the personal circumstances that brought him to the crisis of 1887. Ríos Sánchez sees Unamuno's "conversion" as it is described in the *Diario íntimo* as the beginning of his second stage, one

12. Ríos Sánchez, *El reformador Unamuno*, 9–10.

in which Unamuno would read Protestant theologians for spiritual inspiration, which would in turn engender in him a desire to reform Spanish Catholic religiosity to become more genuinely Christian. He sees this reforming period lasting until 1907, when Unamuno rejects some of his Protestant mentors and returns to a more Catholic stance, which is characterized as "catolicismo popular" ("popular Catholicism"). This is a more personal faith in which Unamuno looks to God as the guarantor of eternal life. This last stage according to Ríos Sánchez is the stage of *Del sentimiento trágico de la vida*. While these stages are fairly well accepted by Unamuno scholars, I would suggest that the relative emphases on Protestantism or Catholicism are already woven around the themes just outlined in the *Diario íntimo*. It is also the case that there is a lot left of Unamuno's story after the writing of *Del sentimiento trágico de la vida*, published in 1913. Let us turn to the life events of the second stage, according to Ríos Sánchez' accounting.

In October of 1900, a shock-wave ran through Salamanca as it became known that Miguel de Unamuno had been named rector of the university. The appointment came from the central government in Madrid and surprised everyone, including Unamuno himself. The central government was conservative and he was a declared socialist. His views had already gotten him into trouble with the local Catholic bishop. He had just given a lecture for the opening of the school year in which he once again excoriated the system of education in Spain. He was only thirty-six years old and he had only had his post for nine years. But he had made his mark, and the new minister of education saw him as open to the renewal and reform that was needed in the educational system.

The new position gave the professor of Greek an even higher profile and a more prestigious platform from which to speak. According to Ríos Sánchez, his desire during these years was to be the Spanish Martin Luther, to bring reform to Spanish Catholicism. Ríos Sánchez quotes from a letter of Unamuno's to his friend Pedro de Múgica in December of 1903, "Desde hace algún tiempo, desde que pasé cierta honda crisis de conciencia, se va afirmando en mí una profundísima persuasión de que soy un instrumento en manos de Dios para contribuir a la renovación espiritual de España. Toda mi vida desde hace algún tiempo, mis triunfos, la popularidad que voy ganando, mi elevación a este rectorado, todo ello me parece enderezado en ponerme en situación tal de autoridad y de prestigio que haga mi obra más fructuosa."[13] ("For some time, since I experienced a certain, deep

---

13. Unamuno, quoted in Ríos Sánchez, *El reformador Unamuno*, 15–16.

YBP Library Services

EVANS, JAN E., 1949-

MIGUEL DE UNAMUNO'S QUEST FOR FAITH: A
KIERKEGAARDIAN UNDERSTANDING OF UNAMUNO'S
STRUGGLE TO...   Paper   138 P.
EUGENE: PICKWICK PUBLICATIONS, 2013

TITLE CONT: BELIEVE. AUTH: BAYLOR UNIV.

ISBN 1620321068   **Library PO#** SLIP ORDERS

		List	18.00	USD
6207 UNIV OF TEXAS/SAN ANTONIO	**Disc**	17.0%		
App. Date 12/04/13 SPN.APR 6108-09	**Net**	14.94	USD	

SUBJ: UNAMUNO, MIGUEL DE, 1864-1936--CRIT. &
INTERPR.

CLASS PQ6639   DEWEY# 868.6209   LEVEL ADV-AC

YBP Library Services

EVANS, JAN E., 1949-

MIGUEL DE UNAMUNO'S QUEST FOR FAITH: A
KIERKEGAARDIAN UNDERSTANDING OF UNAMUNO'S
STRUGGLE TO...   Paper   138 P.
EUGENE: PICKWICK PUBLICATIONS, 2013

TITLE CONT: BELIEVE. AUTH: BAYLOR UNIV.

ISBN 1620321068   **Library PO#** SLIP ORDERS

		List	18.00	USD
6207 UNIV OF TEXAS/SAN ANTONIO	**Disc**	17.0%		
App. Date 12/04/13 SPN.APR 6108-09	**Net**	14.94	USD	

SUBJ: UNAMUNO, MIGUEL DE, 1864-1936--CRIT. &
INTERPR.

CLASS PQ6639   DEWEY# 868.6209   LEVEL ADV-AC

crisis of conscience, a profound persuasion has been affirmed in me that I am an instrument in God's hands to contribute to the spiritual renewal of Spain. All of my life for some time, my triumphs, the popularity that I am winning, my elevation to the rectorship, all of that seems to me to have been set right to put me in a position of authority and prestige that will make my work more fruitful.")

And indeed, Unamuno embarked on a series of what he called *sermones laicos* (secular sermons), denouncing superstition and the "fe del carbonero," that uneducated, unquestioning faith that he abhorred and which he saw as promulgated by Spanish mothers. Though Unamuno doesn't say publically that Protestantism is what Spain needs, he does so in correspondence with Jiménez Ilundain. "Lo del protestantismo no le parece a usted solución eficaz y posible en España. Yo creo que es acaso la única que puede salvarnos de irreligiosismo y de la indiferencia y del olvido de la otra vida."[14] ("Protestantism doesn't seem to you as an effective and possible solution for Spain. I believe that it may be the only one that can save us from irreligiosity and the indifference to and forgetfulness of the other life.") As early as 1903 Unamuno was writing publically about freedom of conscience, a particularly Protestant theme that would resurface throughout his authorship. "El porvenir de España necesita apoyarse en un cimiento religioso, en un modo de concebir y de sentir la vida religiosa y la libertad de conciencia cristiana eternamente distinto al modo como hoy la conciben y sienten los más españoles" (9:882). ("The future of Spain needs to be supported by a religious foundation, in a way of conceiving and feeling religious life and the liberty of Christian conscience eternally distinct from the way that today it is conceived and felt by most Spaniards.")

Ríos Sánchez is very clear about the fact that Unamuno officially had nothing to do with the then extant Iglesia Española Reformada, (Spanish Reformed Church) nor Protestant missionary efforts in Spain, though there are some who have said that he occasionally attended services of that church in Salamanca after 1930. Ríos Sánchez sees a turning away from Protestantism after 1907 when Unamuno distanced himself from Harnack by emphasizing a more Catholic stance on eschatology, the desire for immortality and the continual striving for it, rather than the sureness of the Protestants in their salvation through justification by faith.[15] From 1907 on

14. Ibid., 17.

15. Río Sánchez, *El reformador Unamuno*, 34.

Unamuno would not speak any more about "descatolizando" ("de-catholicizing"), Spain but rather "re-catolizando" ("re-catholicizing") Spain.

Nelson Orringer would say that the "re-catholicizing" of Spain was still very much informed by Unamuno's reading of the Liberal Protestants. His view is that Unamuno was influenced by Hegel and imbued with the positivism found in Krause in his first major work, *En torno al casticismo*, but that after his spiritual crisis in 1887 and the reading of German Liberal Protestants like Schleiermacher, Harnack and Ritschl, as well as French Calvinists like Paul Sabatier, Alexandre-Rodolphe Vinet and Paul Stapfer, Unamuno embraced a Liberal Protestant view in the same time period that Ríos Sánchez calls Unamuno's reforming period.[16] Orringer, in his *Unamuno y los protestantes liberals*, maintains that Unamuno was ultimately a Ritschlian Catholic in what Ríos Sánchez designates as Unamuno's third period, a stance Unamuno most clearly articulates in *Del sentimiento de la vida*.[17] Orringer's careful study is exhaustive in its delving into the texts which Unamuno read, but I hesitate to label Unamuno with Ritschl's name any more than I would label him as a Kierkegaardian, though there are many affinities in the Dane's and the Spaniard's thought.[18]

The difference between "des-catolizando" and "re-catolizando" Spain was apparent to the Catholic hierarchy which criticized Unamuno severely for having expressed the following about his spiritual crisis of 1887 to a correspondent for an anarchist journal. "Bajo aquel golpe interior volví o quise volver a mi antigua fe de niño. ¡Imposible! A lo que realmente he vuelto es a cierto cristianismo sentimental, algo vago, al cristianismo llamado protestantismo liberal" (9:816–17). ("As a result of that interior blow, I returned or tried to return to the old faith of my childhood. Impossible! What I have really returned to is a certain Christian sentimentalism, something vague, like the Christianity of Liberal Protestantism.") The letter was published in November of 1900 without the knowledge or permission of Unamuno, and the reigning bishop of Salamanca and his subordinates began at that point

16. Orringer, Introduction to *Treatise on Love of God*, xv–xxii.

17. Orringer, *Unamuno y los Protestantes Liberales*, 9.

18. The following doctrines of Ritschl found in Unamuno are summarized by Orringer in his "Translator's Introduction" to the *Treatise on Love of God*: "esteem for individual personality as point of departure; preference of practical over theoretical knowledge; an idea of God as love, Will and personality; linking of God to faith, hope, and love; the idea of sin as finite and not meriting punitive measures; the morality of mastery over the world, and the doctrine of love of enemy. Whereas Ritschl is chiefly concerned with forgiveness of sin, Unamuno substitutes his own obsession with salvation after death." 90 n82.

a serious campaign to remove Unamuno from his position as rector, even though Unamuno assured father Cámara that he had never written anything against real religious sentiments and that what he desired more than anything was that Spain completely become Christian.[19] The initial attempt to remove Unamuno was unsuccessful, but it was an omen of things to come.

The years of the rectorship between 1900 and the first half of 1914 were productive ones for the professor of Greek. Unamuno's "obra capital," the most concise compendium of his philosophy, was written during these years first as *Tratado del amor de Dios* (*Treatise on Love of God*), and then published, finally, in 1913 as *Del sentimiento trágico de la vida en los hombres y en los pueblos* (*The Tragic Sense of Life in Men and Nations*).[20] It is interesting to note that even as Unamuno was correcting the proofs for his philosophic work, he was planning to write *El Cristo de Velázquez* whose purpose Unamuno described to a Portuguese poet friend: "A mí me ha dado ahora por formular la fe de mi pueblo, su cristología realista y . . . lo estoy haciendo en verso. Es un poema que se titulará *Ante el Cristo de Velázquez* . . . Quiero hacer una cosa cristiana, bíblica y . . . española. Veremos" (6:24). ("It has been given to me now to formulate the faith of my people, their realistic Christology and . . . I am doing it in verse. It is a poem that will be titled *Before the Christ of Velázquez* . . . I want to make something Christian, biblical and Spanish. We shall see.") The author describes the work to another friend as his best work and his most Catholic work. It is certainly the literary piece that Unamuno spent the most time writing, rewriting and polishing; it was not published until October of 1920. Are its themes different from that of the more philosophic work?

The book length poem takes as its starting point the painting by Diego Velázquez from the seventeeth century that depicts Christ hanging on the cross, his wounds very much in evidence as he hangs his head in death. The poetic voice contemplates the figure awash in light. There are 268 quotes from the Bible in the margins scattered throughout the poem. The poem has been used as devotional material for the faithful and has been condemned as heresy for making Christ too human and not at all divine. The Christ depicted is the source of life, pardon and truth. In poem XII, "Alba" ("Dawn"), Christ's snow white body is the spring or source of all rivers, implying the source of all of life, and thus Christ's body is the peak or summit

19. Rabaté and Rabaté, *Unamuno*, 234.

20. *The Tragic Sense of Life* will be dealt with thoroughly in chapters 3–7, so I will not comment on it here.

of all humanity (6:429). In poem IX, "Sangre" ("Blood"), the poet maintains his gaze on the painting as he writes. The whiteness of the body of Christ becomes an obsession. Here the river of blood contrasts with the whiteness of Christ's body and illumines it. It is the blood of pardon and of forgiveness (6:429). In poem V, "Verdad" ("Truth"), Christ is the truth whose blood washes us from the error of our birth; he is the truth who consoles us in death. He is the torrent of pure water that takes away our thirst. There is very little mention of the resurrection in the entire length of the poem, a fact that supports those who say that this Christ is too human. But here in this one poem about truth, Christ's power to make us live is found in the resurrection. "Eres Tú la Verdad que con su muerte,/ resurrección al fin, nos vivifica" (6:487). ("You are the Truth that with your death,/ ultimate resurrection, gives us life.")

The reader of *El Cristo de Velázquez* can also find the more problematic themes found elsewhere in the Unamunian corpus, the necessity of conflict and the questioning of the meaning of this life if there is no life after death. In poem XXVII, "Espada" ("Sword"), Christ is a sword, and his word is a two edged sword that brings enmity between children and their parents, between brothers and between spouses. Christ is the flame that purifies our hearts, something that only happens through pain and suffering (6:441). In poem VIII, "Saduceismo" ("Sadduceeism"), the poetic voice asks this biblical group that did not believe in the resurrection, "Di, ¿qué es lo que dura?/ . . . ¿qué vida es ésta si esperamos sólo/ a lo que sea cuando no seamos?" (6:490). ("Say, what is it that endures? What sort of life is this one if we only hope for what might be when we are no longer here?") We hear the ongoing struggle with meaning for this life if there is no life after death. In the "Oración final" ("Final Prayer"), that is a continuing cry to this "Hijo de Hombre y Humanidad" ("Son of Man and Humanity"), there is the moment of doubt when the poet uses the subjunctive "*haya*" to emphasize that there is only hope if God exists, "esperanza sólida sobre nosotros mientras haya Dios!" (6:492) ("solid hope about us while there may be God!").

As is the case with so much of Unamuno's work, the mindset with which the reader comes to the text makes all the difference in what he or she gets from it. The faithful see a deep understanding of the suffering of Christ and his work of salvation on the cross. The skeptic sees that this Christ is not a triumphant one, but an agonizing one. Describing the painting in *Del sentimiento trágico de la vida* Unamuno says, "La más alta expresión artística católica, por lo menos española, es en el arte más material, tangible y permanente . . . de la escultura y la pintura, en *El Cristo de Velázquez*, ¡en ese Cristo que está siempre muriéndose, sin acabar nunca de morirse, para darnos vida!" (7:150). ("The highest artistic Catholic expression, at least in Spain, is in the most material, tangible and permanent art . . . of sculpture and painting, of *The Christ of Velázquez,* in this Christ that is always dying, without any end of dying, in order to give us life!") If Christ is always dying, "How can he give life?" the official Catholic Church would ask.

As noted earlier, the local bishop's criticism of Unamuno began almost immediately upon his arrival. In addition to his heterodox theological views, the Church would also be unhappy about his political views, his criticism of the great landowners and his work to reform land ownership. On August 1 of 1914 the local Catholic newspaper ran a headline that said, "A New Rector?" Clearly the locals had advance notice of the announcement that would appear in *La Gaceta de Madrid* on the 30th of the same month. Signed by the king, Alfonso XIII, the decree announced the end of the rectorship of Unamuno and the name of the new rector of the University of Salamanca, Salvador Cuesta y Martín.[21] From all accounts, Unamuno was not informed of his being fired and was never given any cause for the dismissal.

Though Unamuno's dismissal was national news in August of 1914, it paled in importance to the beginning of hostilities of World War I. Quickly the Spanish government moved to declare itself neutral in the conflict. Unamuno was not neutral and had worked with an organization whose stated goal was to oppose German forces already in 1913. In 1917 he signed the Manifesto de la Liga Antigermanófila (Manifesto of the Anti-Germanic League) with other intellectuals that appeared in the nationally distributed *España.* If going against governmental policy had gotten Unamuno fired from his position, it did not deter him from continuing to fight for the Allied cause or any other liberal causes. Unamuno's literary output continued unabated during these years as he wrote *Recuerdos de niñez y de mocedad* and *Abel Sánchez* while he also worked on *El Cristo de Velázquez.* Of his spiritual state he wrote to a friend in 1917 that the spiritual crisis that he had experienced ten years earlier was one from which he had never recovered, nor did he want to recover from it.[22]

Although he began to experience censure in some of the places where he had published before, in the next years Unamuno continued to criticize the king and he narrowed his sights on General Miguel Primo de Rivera.

21. Rabaté and Rabaté, *Unamuno*, 327.

22. Ibid., 367.

In September of 1920, just before the publication of *El Cristo de Velázquez*, Unamuno was tried in a Valencian court for three "crimes of the press," three articles entitled "El archiducado de España" ("The Archduke of Spain"), "Irresponsabilidades" ("Irresponsibilities"), and "La soledad del rey" ("The Loneliness of the King"), which were all published in 1918 and 1919. He was actually sentenced to sixteen years in prison and to pay a fine of 1,000 pesetas.[23] The outcry among the intellectuals for such a breach of the freedom of the press was loud and appeals were set in motion.

Meanwhile Spain entered a disastrous conflict in Morocco that animated more virulent criticism of Alfonso XIII and Primo de Rivera. In May of 1923 Unamuno predicted the coup that established the military dictatorship in September of the same year as he wrote in *España*, "Toda monarquía, todo reino, tiende naturalmente, a la dictadura y al despotism, y más cuando se siente en peligro de muerte."[24] ("All monarchies, every kingdom, naturally tends toward dictatorship and despotism and even more when it feels itself in danger of death.") With increased censure of the press in Spain Unamuno was able to maintain his attack on the dictatorship and its leader in *La Nación* in Argentina, but he was to pay a great price. On the 20th of February of 1924 Unamuno was served the decree of his exile, mandated by Primo de Rivera and affirmed by the king. He was to give up his vice rectorship of the university as well as his teaching post, denying him any salary, and he was to be exiled to Fuerteventura, where he went just one week later. At first the days of exile were tempered with the knowledge of the protests that were happening throughout Spain and Argentina on his behalf. Unamuno was firm in his resolution not to ask for a pardon when he had done nothing wrong. Of the three books that he brought with him, one was his Greek New Testament.

By July Unamuno had managed to arrange for his escape from the island on a French ship called *L'Aiglon* that traveled to Lisbon before going on to France where Unamuno would ultimately be welcomed in Paris. Just days before his escape he received word that he had been pardoned, but he did not trust the drafters of the pardon and purposed not to return to Spain until constitutional guarantees were reinstituted. In Paris he quickly entered into the polemics of what was happening in Spain through writing for *Le Quotidien,* and Primo de Rivera actually responded to his criticism in the same paper, but the French newspaper was banned in Spain. Unamuno

23. Ibid., 403.

24. Unamuno, quoted in Rabaté and Rabaté, *Unamuno*, 438.

had the opportunity to mix with European intellectuals of all stripes and by all accounts had close friends, among them Jean Cassou, who would translate his *Agonía del cristianismo* into French for publication much before it saw the light in Spanish.

In the prologue to the Spanish edition of *Agonía* Unamuno states that this work reiterates what he wrote in *Del sentimiento trágico de la vida* in a more "concrete" and yet more "improvised" form (7:305). What the reader can see is that the book is more improvised than concrete, more mystical than reasoned philosophy. Many of the same themes arise which had defined Unamuno's spiritual journey up to this point, but the text reflects the frustration of his exile and the deepness of his angst as he says, "Este libro fue escrito en París hallándome yo emigrado, refugiado allí, a fines de 1924 . . . presa de una verdadera fiebre espiritual y de una pesadilla de aguardo" (7:305). ("This book was written in Paris where I found myself emigrated and sheltered at the end of 1924 . . . prisoner of a true spiritual fever and of a nightmare of waiting.") Most striking is Unamuno's insistence on struggle as the essence of life and on doubt as the fuel for that struggle. By agony Unamuno means struggle and that is what he proposes to explicate: "Lo que voy a exponer aquí, lector, es mi agonía, mi lucha por el cristianismo, la agonía del cristianismo en mí, su muerte y su resurrección en cada momento de mi vida íntima" (7:308). ("What I am going to expound on here, reader, is my agony, my struggle for Christianity, the agony of Christianity in me, its death and its resurrection in each moment of my intimate life.") He equates his struggle with that of Job, St. Paul, St. Augustine and Pascal. There is solidarity in the struggle with others and one makes oneself in the struggle. Against what is one struggling? Unamuno's answer is "oblivion."

As we saw before, it is the agonizing Christ, the Christ that Unamuno calls the Spanish Christ, which is the one that he upholds. It is not the dead Christ but the Christ who said, "My God, my God, why have you forsaken me?" This is the Christ of the agonizing believer, the one whose faith is alive because, "Fe que no duda es fe muerta" (7:311). ("Faith that does not doubt is dead faith.")

Once again we see the doctrine of *querer creer* as Unamuno repeats the Gospel story of the man who came to Jesus for his son to be healed. When the man was questioned by Jesus, he responded, "I believe, help my unbelief."[25] Unamuno gives a treatise on the difference between *voluntad*

---

25. Mark 9:24 (Revised Standard Version).

(will) to believe and *ganas* (desire) to believe, but the end result is that the agonic faith of which he speaks is one that longs to believe. In his discussion of Pascal, Unamuno attributes to Pascal his own rejection of reason.[26] "¿Creía Pascal? Quería creer. Y la voluntad de creer, la will to believe, como ha dicho William James, otro probabilista, es la única fe posible en un hombre que tiene la inteligencia de las matemáticas, una razón clara y el sentido de la objetividad" (7:346). ("Did Pascal believe? He wanted to believe. And the will to believe, 'the will to believe,' as William James, another probabalist, has said, is the only faith possible in a man who has the intelligence of mathematics, a clear reason and a sense of objectivity.")

What does the agonic struggle accomplish? "El triunfo de la agonía es la muerte, y esta muerte es acaso la vida eterna" (7:334). ("The triumph of agony is death and this death is perhaps eternal life.") The meaning of this life is consumed in struggle and there is no comfort on this side of death. The only glimmer of light is that fellow seekers may learn from the struggle left in the written record of the one in agony. Unamuno claims that Pascal never had peace this side of death. Nevertheless he lives on in those who have read and entered into his world through his work (7:347).

The conclusions of *La agonía del cristianismo* are wholly pessimistic. There is no chapter on love and hope as there is at the end of *Del sentimiento trágico de la vida*. More than once Unamuno compares the agony of Christianity to the agony of western civilization as a whole and more specifically to the agony of Spain. It is understandable that from where he viewed the world in December of 1924 Unamuno used the last words of Christ on the cross to express his own despair, "¡Cristo nuestro, Cristo nuestro! ¿por qué nos has abandonado?" (7:364). ("Our Christ! Our Christ! Why have you abandoned us?")

There would be six long years of exile, but the majority of those would be spent near the Spanish border in Hendaya. In January of 1930 the political winds had changed sufficiently in Spain for Unamuno to be planning his return. Primo de Rivera was dismissed and Unamuno made his triumphal return to Spain in February. In his newly restored position as professor and rector, Unamuno advocated for a new regime, one that would be *laica*, secular, "que no quiere decir irreligiosa, porque cosas de religión pertenecen

---

26. Nelson Orringer says that Unamuno's reading of Pascal was influenced by Alexandre Vinet (1797–1847), a Swiss theologian, and Auguste Sabatier (1839–1901) a French Biblical scholar. *Unamuno y los protestantes liberals*, 48.

a lo más íntimo de la consciencia del hombre,"[27] ("which does not mean irreligious, because the stuff of religion pertains to the most intimate part of the conscience of man.") The Second Republic became a reality in 1931, and Unamuno served as a senator in the Cortes helping to draw up the new constitution. However, he was not in agreement with the stipulation that the instruction of school children should be suddenly secularized. In time, he became very disillusioned with the anticlerical nature of the regime, particularly the sacking of convents and sacred places.

Unamuno had long been a supporter of freedom of religion in general, and particularly of the freedom of Protestants to practice their faith legally. In July of 1922 he had actually presided at a meeting in the Casa del Pueblo de Salamanca organized by Protestants to advocate for the liberty of "cults." According to accounts of the proceedings, Unamuno said that he did not hesitate to say yes to the invitation to preside at the meeting because he always wanted to be with those who were asking for freedom. At the meeting he sounded similar themes about the importance of the liberty of conscience, but it was a liberty that should be used to ask the serious, important religious questions: the meaning of this life and the possibility of the life to come.[28]

It is not surprising then that Unamuno knew and developed a relationship with a Protestant pastor in Salamanca, Atilano Coco, who would figure in the last days of Unamuno in an unexpected way. For unknown offenses, Coco was arrested by Francoist forces in the last days of July of 1936. Coco's wife, Enriqueta Carbonell, asked Unamuno to intercede on her husband's behalf, which he did with the Governor. So confident of his success in helping to free the man, Unamuno appeared at the home of Coco a month after he had been held, expecting to be able to celebrate the man's freedom since he had been assured of his release. Doña Enriqueta recounted the moment many years later in an interview, saying that when Unamuno found out that Coco was still held, he left immediately.[29] Later Coco was accused of being a Mason, and his death seemed imminent. Unamuno carried the letter that Doña Enriqueta wrote with that information into the last, fatal meeting in the Paraninfo at the University of Salamanca when Unamuno denounced the Francoists. It was on the envelope of that letter that he wrote notes from

27. Unamuno, quoted in Rabaté and Rabaté, *Unamuno*, 570.

28. Ríos Sánchez, *El reformador Unamuno*, 111.

29. Ibid., 108.

which he would later declare, "Vencer no es convencer," ("To win is not to convince."), words that would result in his house arrest.[30]

For Unamuno's support of Protestants, their freedom to practice their religion and for Unamuno's advocacy on behalf of Atilano Coco, Protestants to this day revere Unamuno. In 2012, the 75th anniversary of the death of Unamuno, Protestants gathered in Salamanca for various conferences to celebrate the Spanish author whom they claim was very close to them. One of the speakers, Alfredo Pérez Alencart, confidently declared that Unamuno was a Christ follower and a genuine Christian in a television interview in anticipation of the conferences.[31] Catholics throughout Unamuno's life certainly disagreed, and scholars have been mixed in their estimates of what and how much Unamuno believed. The following chapters will attempt to make sense of the essentials of the Unamunian faith clearly and dispassionately, hopefully giving fresh insight to those engaged in the debate and fresh considerations for those who are being introduced to Unamuno for the first time.

During this last period of his life, the period of return and restitution to his life in Salamanca, Unamuno wrote one of his most famous novels, *San Manuel Bueno, mártir.* He himself believed that it was a culminating work, one that encompassed all of the themes that he cared passionately about, saying in the prologue, "tengo la conciencia de haber puesto en ella (la novela) todo mi sentimiento trágico de la vida" (2:1115). ("I have the sense of having put in this novel all of my tragic sense of life.") The story is one of an unbelieving priest who lived such an exemplary life that he is considered for sainthood by the church hierarchy. It is the confession of one of his faithful parishioners who knew the truth, who wanted the truth to be known, but who ultimately questions her own faith and her own version of the story. The novel raises many more questions than it answers, but it focuses on the importance of the central issue with which Unamuno struggled all of his life, the question of whether or not there is life after this one. It is the question that he faced so profoundly that night in March of 1897, the question that defined the focus for all of his literary life, through his absorption of Liberal Protestantism, through his years of political difficulties culminating in his exile and through the years of restitution back in Salamanca.

---

30. Rabaté and Rabaté, *Unamuno,* 684.

31. Hofkamp, "Salamanca acoge a escritores evangélicos con los brazos abiertos," *Protestante Digital.*

In all of his deliberations, scripture was never far from Unamuno's mind and heart. He begins *San Manuel Bueno, mártir* with an epigram from St. Paul that reads, "If only for this life we have hope in Christ, we are of all people most to be pitied."[32] Those readers who are looking for Christian orthodoxy in Unamuno may find it in such references, but there is no avoiding the totality of the struggle that is purposefully never resolved.

32. 1 Corinthians 15:19 (NIV).

3

Truth Must Be Lived

Unamuno and Kierkegaard on "Truth is Subjectivity"

JOHANNES CLIMACUS, A PSEUDONYM of Søren Kierkegaard, claims that "truth is subjectivity" in *Concluding Unscientific Postscript,* and Miguel de Unamuno embraced that claim. Of all the books contained in the fourteen volumes of the first edition of Kierkegaard's collected writings, I believe that *Postscript* was the most influential in Unamuno's thought. The ideas that Climacus outlines in *Postscript* are the ones that resonate most with Unamuno, and they are the ones that make their way into Unamuno's published works, both his philosophical writings and his fiction. There are no less than nine direct quotations from *Postscript* in *Del sentimiento trágico de la vida.* In other places I have explored Unamuno's understanding and use of Climacus' view of "indirect communication."[1] Here I propose to show how Miguel de Unamuno understood the dictum "truth is subjectivity," and how that understanding of Climacus' theme is woven throughout his work.

Climacus says famously that, "*An objective uncertainty, held fast through appropriation with the most passionate inwardness, is the truth,* the highest truth there is for an *existing* person" (CUP 203). There are two major elements of Climacus' statement that are of greatest importance to Unamuno. The first is the notion that in order for truth to matter, it must be lived. Abstract, philosophical speculation is useless. The philosopher must first be an

1. See chapter 1 of *Unamuno and Kierkegaard: Paths to Selfhood in Fiction,* 13–34, and "Passion, Paradox and Indirect Communication: The Influence of *Postscript* on Miguel de Unamuno," 137–52.

existing person. The other is the element of passion, inwardness. Passion is the "how" in the appropriation of truth. Passion leads a person to action and is the means whereby truth becomes lived. It is to a passionate existence that Unamuno wants to awaken his reader. While there is evidence that Unamuno appropriates "truth is subjectivity," there are some clear differences which center on the authors' view of the existence of objective truth. We will see that in embracing Climacus' call for passion without regard to the object of the passion, Unamuno misconstrues Climacus' meaning and promotes a view that is not found in Climacus, much less in Kierkegaard himself.[2] Unamuno is not alone in misconstruing Climacus' meaning.

Thirty years of Kierkegaard scholarship with writers as diverse as Roger Poole[3] and Sylvia Walsh[4] has shown the importance of taking the pseudonymous character of Kierkegaard's corpus seriously. These scholars as well as many others have underscored the fact that in "The First and Last Explanation," which Kierkegaard adds to *Postscript* under his own name, he asks that the ideas and the conclusions of his pseudonyms not be attributed to him. Kierkegaard himself requests, "Therefore, if it should occur to anyone to want to quote a particular passage from the books, it is my wish, my prayer, that he will do me the kindness of citing the respective pseudonymous author's name, not mine" (CUP 627).

Nevertheless, Climacus' claim that "truth is subjectivity" has caused many to identify Kierkegaard as a relativist because they have interpreted "truth is subjectivity" as "truth is subjective." Such a characterization of Kierkegaard's thought is unfortunate and wrongheaded for several reasons. To begin, it is important to note that the Danish is clear. Though the

2. Strictly speaking, *Concluding Unscientific Postscript* should be attributed to Kierkegaard's pseudonym Johannes Climacus rather than to Kierkegaard himself, following Kierkegaard's request in the "First and Last Declaration" attached to *Postscript*. However, it is fairly clear that Unamuno himself did not draw a distinction between Climacus and Kierkegaard as his copy of *Postcript* indicates that he did not read "The First and Last Declaration." In any case, the relation between Climacus and Kierkegaard is a close one, as indicated by the fact that Kierkegaard placed his own name on the title page of *Postscript* as "Editor." Kierkegaard himself tells us in *The Point of View for My Work as An Author* that placing his own name on the title page was a "hint, at least for someone who is concerned with or has a sense for such things" (PV 31–32). Since Climacus does not claim to be a Christian, he cannot simply be identified with Kierkegaard. However, in *The Point of View* Kierkegaard appropriates much of what Climacus has done by claiming that *Postscript* is the turning point of his whole authorship and expresses the crucial issue of the whole authorship: "becoming a Christian" (PV 55).

3. Poole, *Kierkegaard: The Indirect Communication*.

4. Walsh, *Living Poetically: Kierkegaard's Existential Aesthetics*.

adjective *subjektive* (subjective) is used in the title of the relevant chapter, the key passage reads, *"Men Uendelighedens Lidenskab er netop Subjektiviteten og saaledes er Subjektiviteten Sandeden."*[5] ("But the passion of infinity is precisely subjectivity and therefore the truth is subjectivity.") The truth here is identical with the quality designated by the noun "subjectivity" (*Subjektiviteten*) and not by the adjective "subjective" (*subjecktive*). More important is the entire context of this relevant chapter which shows that Climacus' emphasis is not on the existence of multiple truths but rather on the relevance of the truth to the exister.[6] Even if Climacus could be accused of promoting a crass sort of "whatever is true for you is true," one should not attribute that view to Kierkegaard, given Kierkegaard's plea just quoted above. No one should assume that the view of one of Kierkegaard's pseudonyms is identical to his own. However, Climacus himself is not affirming any such crude relativism.

To begin, it is important to recognize that Climacus deals with two sorts of truth at the same time. Their confusion has given rise to misconceptions about Climacus' view of truth. He talks both about "the nature of truth in general" and also about "how an individual can be 'in the truth.'"[7] The first has to do with propositional truth and the second with what makes a life true. The first is abstract, concerned with being in the ideal sense, and the second has to do with how one should live, being in the concrete sense. Both aspects of truth are important to Unamuno. For Climacus truth in the abstract is always an approximation, even if it is tied to what we would call empirical reality. This is so because the object of knowledge is constantly changing, and the person who is attempting to acquire that knowledge is constantly changing as well. Therefore, whatever truth is arrived at must be held modestly, knowing that it will always give way to greater insight and then correction. By underscoring the nature of truth as an approximation, Climacus stresses the fact that the process of acquiring truth is never finished.

What Unamuno takes from Climacus is a view of truth that includes a large emphasis on uncertainty and a rejection of the view that humans ever have the truth as a final possession. Unamuno rails against all who think that they have arrived at the truth. "Para ellos no hay quemantes lágrimas vertidas en silencio, en el silencio del misterio, porque esos bárbaros se lo

---

5. Kierkegaard, *Afsluttende Uvidenskabelig Efterskrift*, 169. Italics original.

6. On this point I rely heavily on a chapter called, "Truth and Subjectivity," in C. S. Evans, *Kierkegaard's* Fragments *and* Postscript," 115–35.

7. Ibid., 116.

creen tener todo resuelto; para ellos no hay inquietud del alma, pues se creen nacidos en posesión de la verdad absoluta" (3:226). ("For them there are no burning tears spilled forth in silence, in the silence of mystery, because these barbarians believe that they have everything resolved; for them there is no restlessness of the soul, because they believe themselves to have been born in possession of the absolute truth.") With Climacus Unamuno wants to hold whatever truth there is modestly, which is one of the reasons that Unamuno speaks out against dogmatism. In the clearest statement we have of Unamuno's purpose for writing he says, "Pero es que mi obra—iba a decir mi misión—es quebrantar la fe de unos y de otros y de los terceros, la fe en la afirmación, la fe en la negación y la fe en la abstención y esto por fe en la fe misma; es combatir a todos los que se resignan, sea al catolicismo, sea al racionalismo, sea al agnosticismo; es hacer que vivan todos inquietos y anhelantes" (7:297–98). ("But it is the fact that my work, I was going to say my mission, is to break the faith of this group and that one and some folks in between, faith in the affirmation, faith in the negation, faith in abstention from faith, and this for the sake of faith in faith itself; it is to combat all those who resign themselves to anything, be it Catholicism, rationalism, or agnosticism; it is to make all people live in longing and disquiet.")

The use of the verb *quebrantar* here is pointed. Unamuno does not say that he wants to destroy faith, faith in the affirmative, faith in the negative, faith in abstention or faith in faith itself. Rather, he wants to *disturb* one's faith in anything. Unamuno does not want anyone to be resigned to a particular dogma because, for him, all of life is a longing that should never be assuaged. "Y el alma, mi alma al menos, anhela otra cosa: no absorción, no quietud, no paz, no apagamiento, sino eterno acercarse sin llegar nunca, inacabable anhelo, eterna esperanza que eternamente se renueva sin acabarse del todo nunca" (7:260). ("And the soul, my soul at least, longs for something else: not absorption, not stillness, not peace, not a quenching, but an eternal coming nearer without ever arriving, insatiable longing, eternal hope that eternally is renewed without ever coming to an end.") Understandably then, he says that it is his purpose to awaken his reader to the need for this longing. "Hay que inquietar los espíritus y enfusar en ellos [los prójimos] fuertes anhelos, aun a sabiendas de que no han de alcanzar nunca lo anhelado" (3:155). ("One must disquiet the spirits [of one's neighbors] and infuse in them powerful longings, even in the knowledge that they will never achieve what they long for.")

Ultimately, uncertainty is the foundation of Unamuno's tragic sense of life. "El escepticismo, la incertidumbre . . . es el fundamento sobre que la desesperación del sentimiento vital ha de fundar su esperanza" (7:172). ("Skepticism, uncertainty, is the foundation on which the heart's despair must build up its hope.") This is the conclusion that Unamuno comes to in chapter 6 of *Del sentimiento trágico de la vida,* after he has surveyed the possibilities that reason affords for meaning in life and found reason bankrupt because it cannot prove that one will survive this life. To reason he juxtaposes the longing for immortality that one's heart declares must be the case but for which there is no rational basis. He then asks for the despair of the heart to embrace the skepticism of reason like a brother and live from the ensuing tension. No compromise is possible from his perspective.

One might reasonably ask, "Is this what Climacus had in mind when he maintained that empirical truth is an approximation?" There is a very important difference between Climacus and Unamuno. When Climacus is discussing the fact that even empirical truth must always be considered an approximation to the truth, he makes an exception. That exception to the presumption of approximation is God, because from the perspective of God, from eternity, truth can be known completely. "For God, presumably because he is eternal and sees from the eternal point of view, truth about empirical actuality may be perfect and not merely approximative."[8] This means that Climacus affirms the existence of objective truth, even if we humans cannot know it in this life.

This exception represents a difference between Climacus and Unamuno. Climacus says, "Existence itself is a system—for God, but it cannot be a system for any existing [*existerende*] spirit" (CUP 118). Climacus assumes that there is truth, truth that is known by God, even if that truth is not available to the exister. Unamuno has no equivalent foundational sense of objective truth found in God. Unamuno equivocates on the existence of God, precisely because His existence cannot be proven rationally. Unamuno's answer to the question "Does God exist?" is that he cannot know. For Unamuno to want to believe is belief, whether or not there is objectively any God to believe in. "[La fe] no es en su esencia sino cosa de voluntad, no de razón, como creer es querer creer, y creer en Dios ante todo y sobre todo es querer que le haya" (7:177). ("[Faith] is not in its essence anything but a matter of the will, not of reason, for to believe is to want to believe and to believe in God before all and over all is to want for him to be.") To

8. Ibid., 118.

define belief as the desire to believe does not sound so very different from Climacus, but Climacus is clear about the object of the desire. He says that the person who seeks to know God subjectively, "at that very moment . . . has God, not by virtue of any objective deliberation but by virtue of the infinite passion of inwardness" (CUP 200). Climacus' emphasis is on the fact that objective truth for humans cannot be gained through speculation but rather through existence, but he does not equivocate about the existence of objective truth. Climacus says, "the god [*Guden*] rescues from delusion the person who in quiet inwardness and honesty before God is concerned for himself; even though he is ever so simple, the god leads him in the suffering of inwardness to the truth" (CUP 615).

Even though Unamuno and Climacus differ on the existence of objective truth, they are in agreement with the fact that truth must be lived. Climacus' foremost concern is the relationship of the truth to the exister. The reason for Climacus starting with the matter of truth in general is to show the limitations of abstract, idealistic thought. For truth to be truth it must affect the existence of the knower. "That the knowing spirit is an existing spirit, and that every human being is such a spirit existing for himself, I cannot repeat often enough" (CUP 189). Unamuno rejects abstract thought in the same way and uses Climacus to make his point. In *Del sentimiento trágico de la vida* Unamuno quotes a very long passage from "Actual and Ethical Subjectivity," which in part says, "But abstraction does not care about whether a particular existing human being is immortal, and just that is the difficulty. It is disinterested, but the difficulty of existence is the existing person's interest, and the existing person is infinitely interested in existing . . . Therefore, when one considered an abstract thinker who is unwilling to make clear to himself and to admit the relation his abstract thinking has to his being and existing person, he makes a comic expression, even if he is ever so distinguished, because he is about to cease to be a human being" (CUP 302).

From the very beginning of *Del sentimiento trágico de la vida*, when speaking of the man "de carne y hueso," ("of flesh and bone,") Unamuno stresses that intellectual posturing and even the pursuit of scientific, empirical truth is worthless unless one balances that knowledge with matters that are important to the heart. "Si un filósofo no es un hombre, es todo menos un filósofo; es, sobre todo, un pedante, es decir, un remedo de hombre" (7:118). ("If a philosopher is not a man he is anything but a philosopher; he is above all a pedant and a pedant is a caricature of a man.") Unamuno gives Descartes as an example of a philosopher who, if he had been successful in his attempt to doubt everything, would have been precisely this sort of pseudo-philosopher, one who put aside the real man who cares about his immortality for the sake of abstraction. As noted in chapter 1, at the end of the chapter titled, "El hombre de carne y hueso," ("The Man of Flesh and Bone,") Unamuno points to models of men in history who are concerned with wisdom of the heart rather than abstract knowledge, and he names Kierkegaard as one of those.

One of the most misunderstood passages of *Postscript* is a famous one in which Climacus juxtaposes two individuals. One is a person living in Christianity with the knowledge of God who enters a church and prays in "untruth." The other is a pagan who prays with passion to an idol. Climacus asks, "Where, then, is there more truth? The one prays in truth to God although he is worshiping an idol; the other prays in untruth to the true God and is therefore in truth worshiping an idol" (CUP 201). Many have concluded that what Climacus is saying here is that there is no objective truth, that truth only depends on the passion with which the truth is held. C. Stephen Evans points out that Climacus is not primarily dealing with propositional truth here; he is asking only about "lived life," about what sort of lived life can be considered to be "true." Evans states, "Climacus is not asserting the absurd thesis that someone can make a false proposition true if only he believes it in the right way . . . He is saying that a person does not exist true-ly by knowing what is objectively true."[9] What is important for Climacus is that a person's existence be transformed by the truth. The truth is realized only when it is acted upon. That person who allows his existence to be permeated by the truth can be said to be "in the truth." In order to make his point, Climacus assumes that the pagan's view is false, but in so doing, he wants to underscore the fact that even though the pagan's view is false, there may be some truth in his life. Climacus' view that there is objective truth—both truth about God and truth for God—is crucial here.

In an essay of 1906, "¿Qué es verdad?" ("What is Truth?"), it would seem that Unamuno understands the import of Climacus' claim here. In it he excoriates those who would abstract truth into divisions like metaphysical, logical and moral truth with impenetrable definitions. For Unamuno the only truth that matters is moral truth and that is the case because it is lived truth. In a challenge to the official Catholic Church that is reminiscent of Kierkegaard's attack on the Danish Lutheran Church, Unamuno declares that the statement that Spain is a Catholic country is a lie. Neither those

9. Ibid., 126.

who are in power nor many who attend mass know what they believe, and the evidence is that their lives are not any different as a result of their beliefs. Climacus says something very similar, and Unamuno underlined it. "If the individual is not changed and continually changed within himself, the introducing of Christianity into a country is no more a religious action than the conquering of countries" (CUP 433). Unamuno points out that many say that they believe the teachings of the Holy Mother Church, but they are really ignorant of those teachings. He says, "En medicina puede curarme la ciencia de mi médico, aunque yo no sepa ni hacia dónde me cae el hígado; pero en religión no puede salvarme la fe de mi confesor. En la vida del espíritu sólo mi verdad me salva, y mi verdad no es la verdad que desconozco, aunque sea ésta la verdad de los demás" (3:863). ("In medicine the science of my doctor can cure me, although I don't know where my liver is; but in religion, the faith of my confessor cannot save me. In the life of the spirit only my truth saves me, and my truth cannot be the truth I do not know, though it may be the truth of others.") With as much fervor as Kierkegaard, Unamuno states that so long as the lie that Spain is a Catholic country is perpetuated, Spain will not be Christian.

The spirit of the passage mentioned above about the Christian and the pagan is evident in this essay on truth. At the beginning Unamuno states, "Vale más el error en que se cree que la realidad en que no se cree" (3:855). ("The error that one believes has more worth than the reality in which one does not believe.") I will go so far as to say that Unamuno had the vision of the Christian and the pagan in mind when he says that the person who cannot conceive of God intellectually, but who longs for him to exist and so orders his life to reflect that desire, believes in God much more than the person who gives intellectual assent but whose life is completely unchanged.

The conclusion of the essay, "¿Qué es verdad?" ("What is Truth?"), would seem to conform to Climacus' view of truth. For truth to be truth, it requires passion and action. "Y bien, en resumen: ¿qué es verdad? Verdad es lo que se cree de todo corazón y con toda el alma. ¿Y qué es creer algo de todo corazón y toda el alma? Obrar conforme a ello" (3:864). ("Now, in summary, what is truth? Truth is what one believes with all of his heart and soul. And what is it to believe something with all of one's heart and soul? To work and live in a way that conforms to that belief.") However, there is a significant difference between Climacus's view of truth and Unamuno's. Unamuno here does not deal with the question of whether or not there is objective truth, but in *Del sentimiento trágico de la vida* he does. There

Unamuno quotes directly from the passage in *Postscript* about the Christian and pagan praying, though his Spanish makes it more of a paraphrase than a translation. "Si de dos hombres—dice Kierkegaard—reza el uno al verdadero Dios con insinceridad personal, y el otro con la pasión toda de la infinitud reza a un ídolo, es el primero el que en realidad ora a un ídolo, mientras que el segundo ora en verdad a Dios" (7:214). ("If of two men, Kierkegaard says, one prays to the true God with personal insincerity, and the other prays with the passion of infinity to an idol, it is the first who prayed in reality to an idol and the second who prays in truth to God.")[10] What is interesting is the fact that Unamuno goes on to correct Climacus, or perhaps say what he wished Climacus had said. "Mejor es decir que es Dios verdadero Aquel a quien se reza y se anhela de verdad" (7:214). ("Better to have said that the true God is the one to whom one prays and the one for whom one truly longs.") For Unamuno the true God is the one who is the focus of his attention. Does this God exist objectively outside a person's experience of him?

Unamuno indicates that God's existence is dependent on our experience of him when he says, "Ese en que crees, lector, ése es tu Dios, el que ha vivido contigo en ti y nació contigo y fue niño cuando eras tú niño, y fue haciéndose hombre según tú te hacías hombre y que se te disipa cuando te disipas" (7:215). ("The one in whom you believe, that one is your god, he who has lived with you and in you and was born with you and was a child when you were a child, and continued to become a man when you became a man and who disappears when you disappear.") In other words, the God you believe in dies when you die. But then he seems to echo Saint Augustine when he says, "Y este Dios, el Dios vivo, tu Dios, nuestro Dios, está en mí, está en ti, vive en nosotros, y nosotros vivimos, nos movemos y somos en El. Y está en nosotros por el hambre que de El tenemos, por el anhelo, haciéndonos apetecer" (7:214). ("And this God, the God who is alive, your God, our God, is in me and is in you and he lives in us and we live and we move and we are in Him. And he is in us because of the hunger that we have of him by means of the longing, making us hungry.") In this case it

10. The Hong translation in English has the passage, "If someone who lives in the midst of Christianity enters, with knowledge of the true idea of God, the house of God, the house of the true God, and prays but prays in untruth, and if someone lives in an idolatrous land but prays with all the passion of infinity, although his eyes are resting upon the image of an idol—where, then, is there more truth? The one prays in truth to God although he is worshiping an idol; the other prays in untruth to the true God and is therefore in truth worshiping an idol" (CUP 201).

is God, clearly a being outside myself, who creates in me a "God shaped hollow" that causes the longing that can only be filled by himself. It is not unlike Unamuno to consciously speak in paradoxical terms about those concepts that are difficult to grasp. He does not want to come down on one side of this issue of whether or not there is objective truth or whether God exists. He wants to live in the tension of the difficulties of knowing, as he indicates in the last paragraphs of this same chapter, "¿Existe Dios? Esa persona eternal y eternizadora que da sentido . . . al Universo, ¿es algo sustancial fuera de nuestra consciencia, fuera de nuestro anhelo? He aquí algo insoluble, y vale más que así lo sea. Bástele a la razón el no poder probar la imposibilidad de su existencia. Creer en Dios es anhelar que le haya y es, además, conducirse como si le hubiera; es vivir de ese anhelo y hacer de él nuestro íntimo resorte de acción" (7:218–19). ("Does God exist? That person who is eternal and eternalizing who gives meaning . . . to the universe, is he something substantial outside of our consciousness, outside of our longing? Here we have what is insoluble and it seems so because it should be that way. Let it be enough that reason cannot prove the impossibility of his existence. To believe in God is to long that he exists and even more, to conduct oneself as if he existed; it is to live from this longing and to make of it our ultimate resource of action.") So to believe in God is to long for him to exist. That is enough to make him the source of our actions.

While Unamuno's ultimate plea is for the existing person to long for God's existence and live as though God exists, he leaves the question of God's existence "insoluble." Going back to the passage about the Christian and the pagan, Climacus does not say that the person praying in the passion of infinity to the idol is praying to the true God, as Unamuno translates the passage. Rather, Climacus asks, "Where is there more truth?" The point is having the "right" belief in the true God is worthless if that belief is not lived. And his point is not that the pagan's beliefs are true, but that the pagan himself has "more truth" in his life. In order to arrive at objective truth, one must come at it subjectively. But Climacus does assume that there is objective truth to be known when he says, "Just as important as the truth, and of the two the even more important one, is the mode in which the truth is accepted" (CUP 247).

The last element of "truth is subjectivity" that must be explored if one is to understand Unamuno's reception of Climacus' view is the element of passion. For Climacus passion is the link between abstract speculation and true existence. One may speculate about multiple possibilities, but those possibilities hold no truth for the individual until the individual stops the speculative process and takes a step, a leap, that puts one into action. Climacus says, "reflection can be stopped only by a leap" (CUP 115). It is passion that impels and empowers the exister to choose and to act on that choice. Unamuno underlined the following in *Postscript* that concludes the paragraph about the necessity of the leap. "Yet it is assumed that reflection can stop itself objectively, whereas it is just the other way around; reflection cannot be stopped objectively, and when it is stopped subjectively it does not stop of its own accord, but it is the subject who stops it" (CUP 115). In order for the truth to be appropriated in inwardness, the individual stops the speculation and takes the leap, the step that leads to action.

It would seem that Unamuno embraces such a view of passionate action in the "¿Qué es verdad?" ("What is Truth?") essay as quoted above. He maintains there that truth is what the heart believes and puts into action, action in accordance with the belief. Further, in the essay entitled "El sepulcro de Don Quijote," ("The Tomb of Don Quixote") that Unamuno placed at the beginning of the second edition of *Vida de Don Quijote y Sancho*, (*Life of Don Quixote and Sancho*) he makes a sweeping statement that seems to hold true for many of his protagonists, and therefore we can take seriously as a foundational statement from the author: "Procura vivir en continuo vértigo pasional, dominado por una pasión cualquiera. Sólo los apasionados llevan a cabo obras verdaderamente duraderas" (3:58). ("Try to live in continual passion, dominated by any passion. Only those who are passionate bring about works that are really enduring.") The context here is the story of Don Quixote, and Unamuno reveres him because of his passion. Don Quixote's passion is the model for Unamuno's protagonists as we can see at the end of the Prologue to *San Manuel Bueno, mártir*, where Unamuno equates Don Manuel, the priest protagonist, and Don Quixote (2:1123). For Unamuno both Don Quixote and Don Manuel Bueno live "in the truth" because they have appropriated their truth in the passion of inwardness that leads to action. They both "carry out works that are truly enduring." Don Quixote rights the wrongs that he perceives, even though others do not perceive them in the same way. Don Manuel, the priest, gives his life in service to his parishioners with absolute passion, even though he cannot believe.

As we saw earlier, Unamuno sees as his work, his mission, the task of waking his reader to passionate existence. In part, Unamuno was calling for his reader to care passionately about immortality, which follows logically from another quote from *Postscript* which Unamuno underlined. "But the expression for the utmost exertion of subjectivity is the infinitely passionate interest in its eternal happiness" (CUP 53). As we shall see in chapter 4, for Unamuno the question of immortality is the central question for all of us, and it is the one that we should care most passionately about. He challenges others to share that passion by saying, "Sólo los débiles se resignan a la muerte final y sustituyen con otro el anhelo de inmortalidad personal" (3:139). ("Only the weak resign themselves to final death and substitute something else for the longing for personal immortality.")

The desire for perpetuity is the passion that overcomes doubt, but it should be noted that Unamuno's sense of "overcoming doubt" is very unlike that of Climacus. Unamuno wants to retain skepticism and doubt just as passionately as he declares that one must, with the heart, long for immortality. He calls for maintaining the tension between reason and feeling, the head and the heart. He says that it is not the Cartesian doubt that he is advocating, but another, passionate doubt. "Esta otra duda es una duda de pasión, es el eterno conflicto entre la razón y el sentimiento, la ciencia y la vida, la lógica y la biótica" (7:173). ("This other doubt is a doubt of passion, it is the eternal conflict between reason and feeling, science and life, logic and biotic.") Furthermore, he builds his entire tragic sense of life on that passionate doubt. "Es el conflicto mismo, es la misma apasionada incertidumbre lo que unifica mi acción y me hace vivir y obrar" (7:62). ("It is conflict itself, the same passionate uncertainty that unifies my actions and makes me live and work.")

Climacus would describe what Unamuno is advocating as "opposite passions" and not the sort of "leap" he is demanding. For Climacus, the leap in passion precludes speculative doubt. He says in *Philosophical Fragments*, "Belief is the opposite of doubt. Belief and doubt are not two kinds of knowledge that can be defined in continuity with each other, for neither of them is a cognitive act, and they are opposite passions. Belief is a sense for coming into existence, and doubt is a protest against any conclusion that wants to go beyond immediate sensation and immediate knowledge" (PF 84).[11]

There are important differences to note here. Even though Unamuno calls for passionate action, he retains the right to doubt and not come to any conclusion. Though he says that faith in immortality is irrational, he wants to retain reason. "Razón y fe son dos enemigos que no pueden sostenerse el uno sin el otro" (7:175). ("Reason and faith are two enemies who cannot

---

11. One should note that the Danish term for "belief" here (*Tro*), can also be translated as "faith."

exist one without the other.") He wants the struggle between faith and reason to be the basis of spiritual life. "La paz entre estas dos potencias se hace imposible, y hay que vivir de su Guerra. Y hacer de ésta de la Guerra misma, condición de nuestra vida espiritual" (7:172). ("Peace between these two powers is impossible. And one must live from their war. And to make of this selfsame war the condition of our spiritual life.") Climacus would reject Unamuno's view as one that would, in fact, keep the individual from living "in the truth," because speculation would not really have been stopped.

Climacus would also reject Unamuno's injunction to "seek to live in continuous, passionate vertigo, dominated by whatever passion." As has been noted before, Climacus does not advocate what others have attributed to him in the telling of the story of the Christian and the pagan. He is not saying that whatever "truth" that is held passionately is objectively true. For Climacus, and even more clearly for Kierkegaard, there is an objective truth, and it matters greatly which passions you acquire. Climacus' point in saying that "truth is subjectivity" is that subjective truth will lead ultimately to objective truth. Kierkegaard himself comments on Climacus' work, "In all the usual talk that Johannes Climacus is mere subjectivity, etc., it has been completely overlooked that in addition to all his other concretions he points out in one of the last sections that the remarkable thing is that there is a "How" with the characteristic that when the "How" is scrupulously rendered the "What" is also given, and this is the How of "faith"(JP 4550). The "What" that is also given is not part of Unamuno's view of truth, and this sort of Kierkegaardian faith that is grounded in a God who is there, and not just longed for, is not shared by Unamuno.

To conclude, there is much in Climacus' view that "truth is subjectivity" that is attractive to Unamuno. We have seen from his more philosophical works like "¿Qué es verdad?" *Del sentimiento trágico de la vida,* and *La vida de Don Quijote y Sancho,* that Unamuno appropriates two important elements of Climacus' view: 1) in order for truth to be truth it must be lived and 2) the necessary movement from abstraction to action is found in passion. Unamuno's appropriation of Climacus' thought can be summed up in a passage Unamuno underlined in *Postscript* which he quotes in *Del sentimiento trágico de la vida.* Unamuno uses the quote to underscore the bankruptcy of rationalism and the vitality of passion. "If it were the same with thinkers in our day, pure thinking would have led to one suicide after another, because suicide is the only existence-consequence of pure thinking...We do not praise suicide, but certainly the passion. Now, however a thinker is a creature worth seeing, who at certain times of the day is singularly ingenious but otherwise has nothing in common with a human being" (CUP 308).[12] Both Climacus and Unamuno recognize the need for truth to be lived passionately for a person truly to be a human being. Let us now turn to the truth that matters above all else for Unamuno, the truth of our death and the question of what happens when we die.

12. Unamuno, *Del sentimiento trágico,* 7:178.

4

Unamuno's Passion for Immortality

Narcissism or Foundation for Religious Belief?

IT IS NOT AN exaggeration to say that Miguel de Unamuno was obsessed with the question of whether or not there is life after death. Should that be surprising for an author who is most often identified with the Generation of 1898? For some time the Generation of '98 was defined as those authors in Spain who sought to reinterpret their national identity after the disastrous loss of the remnants of Spanish colonial power in the Spanish American War. However, the categorization of this group of writers has been found to be limiting and erroneous on the basis of historical fact, since the sense of societal decadence and the cultural malaise that resulted has been traced to far before "El Desastre" ("The Disaster"). But it is also the case, as Pedro Cerezo Galán has shown in *El mal del siglo* (*The Evil of the Century*), that the authors of '98 participated in what he calls the "spirit of the age," that swept over all of Europe. It was an age in which confidence in the industrial age, fueled by positivism and a trust in science devolved into nihilism as a "hermeneutic," when science, progressivism and revolution were found to have no unifying vision of the world to replace that of religion in earlier times.[1]

The Spanish writers of the turn of the century participated with others across Europe in a "fatigue" of intellectualism that combined with a "metaphysical sadness."[2] In fact, Unamuno himself links the center of his

1. Cerezo Galán, *El mal del siglo*, 19–20.
2. Ibid., 49.

concerns with the rest of Europe when he says, "Y la famosa *maladie du siècle* que se anuncia en Rousseau y acusa más claramente que nadie el *Obermann* de Sénancour, no era otra cosa que la pérdida de la fe en la inmortalidad del alma, en la finalidad humana del Universo" (7:284). ("The famous *maladie du siècle* (world-weariness) that is announced in Rousseau and which the *Obermann* of Sénacour declared more clearly than anyone to be nothing other than the loss of faith in the immortality of the soul, in the human finality of the Universe.")

It is not surprising, then, that the bulk of Unamuno's life's work is bound up in a universal concern that goes far beyond the borders of his particular national identity—the question of what happens to our individual selves when we die.[3] In "Soledad" ("Solitude") he says, "La cuestión humana es saber que habrá de ser de mi conciencia, de la tuya, de la del otro y de la de todos, después de que cada uno de nosotros se muera" (1:1253). ("The human question is to know what will happen to my consciousness, to yours, to that of the other and to that of everyone, after each and every one of us dies.") In *Del sentimiento trágico de la vida* Unamuno himself claims that this question, the question of what happens when we die, is the basis of all philosophy and religion.

As we saw in chapter 2, Unamuno's own personal crisis, the spiritual crisis of 1897 that caused Unamuno to question the positivism which he had absorbed as a university student, predated "El Desastre." The *Diario íntimo*, written between 1897 and 1902, documents Unamuno's attempt to recover faith, the faith of his childhood and the faith that he knew could answer the question of immortality that tormented his soul. The manuscript for the *Diario* was not found until 1957, and it seems as though Unamuno never intended for it to be published.

In the *Diario* are all of the contradictions that make up Unamuno's personality and his philosophical framework. The tension between faith and reason is played out as the struggle between the life force that keeps one living and the demands of reason. The challenge of surrendering one's will to God strives against the pride of a doubtful mind. Unamuno's struggle with the end of life is a very personal contest, though the question of our eternal end is a universal concern, and Unamuno believed that there were too many people

---

3. Sánchez Barbudo, *Estudios sobre Unamuno y Machado*, 227, quotes from a letter by Unamuno to Pedro Ilundain of December 23, 1898 that says, "Pero la verdad es que estos dramas nacionales me interesan mucho menos que los que se desarrollan en la conciencia de cada uno." ("But the truth is that these national dramas interest me much less than those that are developed in the conscience of each one.")

who had not properly thought about it. In fact, he saw his life's work as one of awaking his readers to wrestle with the complexity of the problem.

The question of the meaning of existence worked its way into everything Unamuno wrote, not just his essays and philosophical work but also his plays, his novels, and his poetry.[4] Given the overwhelming presence of death in his writings, one might justifiably ask, was Unamuno's desire for immortality merely a narcissistic need that his own precious essence not pass from this earth? One would be tempted to say "yes," when one looks at Unamuno's attempts at immortality through his writing, his "hijos espirituales" ("spiritual children"), and his constant worry about his own reputation.[5] There is no doubt that Unamuno reveals much about his own insecurities and personal limitations through his ruminations on whether or not life after death can be conceived. Nevertheless, Unamuno's struggle rings true for the contemporary person who faces up to his or her own mortality. And even if his journey is self-absorbed and at times narcissistic to a fault, his revelations can be helpful to a fellow traveler.

In order to understand Unamuno's desire for immortality, we must first understand the nature of the self that he wants to preserve. I will then explore Unamuno's struggle to believe, his own questioning of his desire to live forever and how that desire treads on the boundaries of personal vanity and self-absorbed pride. In the process we will see the possible ways of gaining immortality that Unamuno considers. Ultimately, we will see how all of the ways of gaining immortality fail, save the one that requires the existence of God as the guarantor of the possibility of immortality.[6] To be able to believe in such a God Unamuno appropriates something like Wil-

---

4. Clemencia Forero Ucros claims in her article, "El deseo de inmortalidad en don Miguel de Unamuno," 50, that the relationship of Unamuno to his work is that "Sus creaciones deben servirle de pasaporte a la inmortalidad," ("His creations should serve him as a passport to immortality.") She demonstrates her thesis particularly through Unamuno's poetry.

5. Thomas Franz ably demonstrates the extent to which Unamuno was successful in using his characters to achieve his own immortality in "Parenthood, Authorship and Immortality in Unamuno's Narratives."

6. Santiago Juan-Navarro, in his article, "La reflexión sobre la inmortalidad en la obra de Unamuno: Filosofía de la existencia, epistemología y pensamiento religioso," identifies several variants on the theme of immortality in the work of Unamuno as though they were all equally important, for example, the struggle to survive through family, work and literature along with the resurrection of the body. I see the first three as alternatives necessitated when the last is subverted by Unamuno's need to keep reason in tension with faith.

liam James's "will to believe." Finally we will make some judgments about the use that Unamuno makes of his own proof for God's existence, and whether he was able to believe in it or not.

Unamuno famously begins his major philosophical work, *Del sentimiento trágico de la vida*, with a chapter on "El hombre de carne y hueso" "The Man of Flesh and Bone." First and foremost, Unamuno underscores that "ser un hombre es ser algo concreto, unitario y substantivo, es ser cosa, *res*" (7:112). ("to be a man is to be something concrete, unitary, substantial; it is to be a thing.") This concrete man of substance has a unity in space and has continuity in time. Change happens in a person over the course of a lifetime, but that change must happen within the person's substantial continuity.

Unamuno quotes Spinoza as saying, "Cada cosa, en cuanto es en sí, se esfuerza por perseverar en su ser" (7:112). ("Everything, in so far as it is in itself, endeavors to persist in its own being.") He explains Spinoza's claim as our personal desire to continue to live as human persons and that "este anhelo de nunca morirnos es nuestra esencia actual" (7:113). ("this longing to never die is our essential essence.") However, the form of the being that will persist must be individual and not merely part of an undifferentiated cosmos. In a chapter entitled "El hambre de inmortalidad" ("The Hunger for Immortality"), Unamuno says that there is no consolation in believing that all of the matter and the energy in the universe is never lost and is only transformed in one way or another. What is significant is the individual's particular matter and energy. He says that monism is a deception and that what we want is to be the individual substance that we are now.

In the *Diario* Unamuno calls "triste consuelo" ("sad comfort") the suggestion that all of our ideas, the mental and spiritual results of our labor, are never lost since they continue to contribute to progress (8:835). In *Del sentimiento tragico de la vida* he also points out that pantheism is of no help for the immortality of the individual soul. To believe that we were part of God before we were born and return to him when we die is to extinguish any sense of individual consciousness (7:161). It is instructive to note that Unamuno's fear here is a fear of becoming nothing, not a fear of hell. In the *Diario íntimo* he says, "Mi terror ha sido el aniquilamiento, la anulación, la nada más allá de la tumba" (8:793). ("My terror has been annihilation, obliteration, the nothingness beyond the tomb.") He says that if he were to be in hell and suffer, he would at least know that he existed. But he doesn't believe in hell; it was one of the first of his childhood beliefs that he gave up.

This desire to live is all consuming. "No quiero morirme, no; no quiero, ni quiero quererlo; quiero vivir siempre, siempre, siempre, y vivir yo, este pobre yo que me soy y me siento ser ahora y aquí y por esto me tortura el problema de la duración de mi alma, de la mía propia" (7:136). ("I don't want to die, no, not at all; neither do I want to want to die; I want to live always, always, always, and for me to live, this poor I that I am and that I feel myself to be here and now, and therefore the problem of the duration of my soul tortures me, of my very own soul.") Why is this substantial me so important? Why is this desire to continue into eternity so important? Because if all there is to me is this life, then there is no meaning in life. Simply put, "Si muero, ya nada tiene sentido" (7:129). ("If I die, nothing makes sense now.") The same sentiment expressed in the *Diario* reads, "Si yo desaparezco del todo, si desaparece mi conciencia personal, con ella desaparece para mí el mundo. Si mi yo no es más que un fenómeno pasajero, un fenómeno pasajero es el mundo en que vivo" (8:835). ("If I disappear from everything, if my personal consciousness disappears, with it the world disappears for me. If my "I" is no more than a passing phenomenon, so also is the world in which I live a passing phenomenon.") So the stakes are high. In order to live now, I need to believe that I will live after my death. And the "I" that will live will be recognizably me, my individual consciousness. When reacting to an imagined objection that his desire for immortality is just "hediondo orgullo," "foul smelling pride," Unamuno declares, "No reclamo derecho ni merecimiento alguno; es sólo una necesidad, lo necesito para vivir" (7:137). ("I do not claim any right or merit at all; it is only a necessity, I need it in order to live.") Unamuno recognizes that belief in a life after death must involve some sort of resurrection, and that the topic of resurrection is offensive to rational minds, pointing to the reaction of the Athenians to the Apostle Paul's speaking to them about the resurrection from the dead. To the "reasonable" crowd that would say that his obsession is madness or a disease he says, "¡No! No me someto a la razón y me rebelo contra ella" (7:139). ("No! I do not submit myself to reason and I rebel against it.") But it is reason and its demands to which Unamuno must come back again and again. He cannot dismiss it easily, and it will pursue him for his entire life.

In the *Diario* Unamuno sets out the path from intellectualism that leads through nothingness to God. "La razón humana, abandonada a sí misma, lleva al absoluto fenomenismo, al nihilismo . . . La nada es inconcebible. Y así se cae en Dios, y se revela su gloria brotando de la desolación de la nada . . . la razón combina y analiza, la fe crea" (8:795). ("Human reason, abandoned to itself leads to absolute phenomenalism, to nihilism . . . Nothingness is inconceivable. And therefore one falls into God, and his glory is revealed, springing from the desolation of nothingness . . . Reason combines and analyzes; faith creates.") The path from intellectualism to God is only achieved through humility. "Por la humildad se alcanza la sabiduría de los sencillos, que es saber vivir en paz consigo mismo y con el mundo, en la paz del Señor, descansando en la verdad y no en la razón" (8:780). ("Through humility one achieves the wisdom of the simple folk, which is knowing how to live with yourself and with the world in the peace of the Lord, resting in the truth and not in reason.") And what is the truth in which one can rest? Unamuno centers on the essence of Christianity when he states that in Christ's resurrection is the promise of our individual resurrection, emphasizing the scripture passage from Corinthians 15 that begins Unamuno's novel about the unbelieving priest, *San Manuel Bueno, mártir*, and also appears here in this section of *Del sentimiento trágico de la vida*. It reads, "Si sólo en esta vida esperamos en Cristo, somos los más miserables de los hombres todos" (2:1127; 7:146). ("If for this life only we have hope in Christ, we are of all men most to be pitied.")

Unamuno judges Liberal Protestantism for its embrace of higher Biblical criticism in the nineteenth century when he says, "Entre los protestantes, este Jesús histórico sufre bajo el escalpelo de la crítica, mientras vive el Cristo católico, el verdaderamente histórico, el que vive en los siglos garantizando la fe en la inmortalidad y la salvación personales" (7:147). ("Among the Protestants, this historical Jesus suffers under the scalpel of criticism, while the Catholic Christ lives, the truly historical one, he who lives throughout the centuries guaranteeing faith in immortality and personal salvation.") The Protestant higher criticism of the historicity of the Bible has taken away the divinity of Christ and therefore any hope that belief in Christ's redemption would have anything to do with our eternal fate. But Unamuno also sharply criticizes the official Catholic Church for turning faith into dogma, reducing faith to a series of rational arguments for God's existence. Unamuno decries the fact that, "Y ya no basta creer en la existencia de Dios, sino que cae anatema sobre quien, aun creyendo en ella, no cree que esa su existencia sea por razones demostrable o que hasta hoy nadie con ellas la ha demostrado irrefutablemente" (7:154). ("And it is no longer enough to believe in the existence of God, but rather anathema falls on the person who, believing in it, doesn't believe that the existence of God can be demonstrated rationally, or that until now, no one has demonstrated it irrefutably with reason.") The unintended but inevitable result of such rationalization is that the Church requires the believer with a questioning mind to set aside any doubts and swallow the entire dogma or believe nothing at all. Unamuno concludes, "La solución católica de nuestro problema, de nuestro único problema vital, del problema de la inmortalidad y salvación eterna del alma individual, satisface a la voluntad y, por lo tanto, a la vida; pero al querer racionalizarla con la teología dogmática, no satisface a la razón" (7:155). ("The Catholic solution to our problem, our unique vital problem, the problem of immortality and eternal salvation of the individual soul, satisfies the will and therefore, life; but upon wanting to rationalize the solution with dogmatic theology, it does not satisfy reason.")

So we can see that there is no doubt that Unamuno understands the biblical, Christian answer to the question of immortality, and he says that it does satisfy the will and life, but it does not stand up to intellectual questioning, reason in general. Herein lies the fundamental contradiction. Unamuno says that science or reason can never satisfy the needs of our heart because most importantly, neither can ever satisfy our need for immortality. Reason shows that we will all die. "La verdad racional y la vida están en contraposición . . . la razón humana, dentro de sus límites, no sólo no prueba racionalmente que el alma sea inmortal . . . sino que prueba más bien . . . que la conciencia individual no puede persistir después de la muerte del organismo corporal de que depende" (8:171). ("Rational truth and life are in opposition . . . human reason, within its limits, not only does not rationally prove that the soul is immortal, rather, it does prove that the individual consciousness cannot persist after the death of the bodily organism on which it depends.") If faith in the Christian God is not possible and reason shows that our individual conscience will not outlive our death, then the individual will seek other means to make himself live on after he dies.

In the *Diario* Unamuno deals with the possibility of our living on in our children and at least leaving one's name to be remembered forever. He asks if the memory we have of loved ones who are now gone will remain after we die. Since it seems as though their memory dies with us, so will the memory of our name be gone soon enough. He then speculates that his fictional characters will be remembered long after he is remembered, just as the fame of Don Quijote is much more than his author, Cervantes (8:785). He worries about his own need to make a name for himself even in the church (8:818). He calls the desire for immortality to be achieved through children and works, "sad comfort," if, in fact, there is no life after death (8:848).[7]

7. In *Tratado del amor de Dios*, 582. Unamuno says, "Cuando las dudas nos invaden y

Unamuno fights his own need for his name and fame to live after his death. He even questions his own motivation for being fixed on the question of death and eternity. "Cuando esa idea de la muerte, que hoy paraliza mis trabajos y me sume en tristeza e impotencia, sea la misma que me impulse a trabajar por la eternidad de mi alma, no por *inmortalizar* mi nombre entre los mortales, entonces estaré curado" (8:807). ("When the idea of death that today paralyzes and consumes me in sadness and impotence comes to be the motivation for working for the eternity of my soul and not the *immortalizing* of my name among mortals, then I will be cured.") But it seems that Unamuno will never be cured.[8]

Since there is such a clear and compelling answer to the question of immortality in the Christ of Christianity, why can't Unamuno put aside the doubts of the intellect? A reading of the *Diario* shows that Unamuno understood what it would take to do so. It also reveals a vacillation between faith and reason that is wrenching at every turn.[9]

On the very first page of the *Diario* Unamuno states that the truth can only be found with humility and not with reason (8:777). Humility allows one to surrender to God and his son, Jesus Christ. Unamuno recognizes that it is reason that keeps one from being humble when he says, "Hay que perderse en esa nada que nos aterra para llegar a la vida eterna y serlo todo. Sólo haciéndonos nada llegaremos a serlo todo; sólo reconociendo la nada de nuestra razón, cobraremos por la fe el todo de la verdad" (8:801). ("One must lose oneself in that nothingness that terrorizes us in order to achieve eternal life, and to be it completely. Only by making ourselves nothing will we achieve it fully, only by recognizing the nothingness of our reason will we

---

nublan la fe en la inmortalidad del alma, cobra brío y doloroso empuje el ansia de perpetuar el nombre, de alcanzar una sobra de inmortalidad siquiera. Y de aquí esa tremenda lucha por singularizarse, por sobrevivir de algún modo en otros" (582). ("When doubts invade us and cloud faith in the immortality of the soul, it takes its toll on the spirit, and painfully pushes the desire to perpetuate one's name, to achieve some semblance of some sort of immortality. And from there this tremendous struggle to distinguish oneself, to survive by some means in others.")

8. While the *Diario* expresses a desire to be healed, in *Vida de don Quijote y Sancho* Unamuno talks about the need for the wound to be left open so that the longing for eternity can never be assuaged (3:241). The idea of the unhealed wound will be explored in chapter 6.

9. By the time of the publication of *Del sentimiento trágico de la vida* Unamuno states unapologetically, "Esa sed de vida eterna apáganla muchos, los sencillos sobre todo, en la fuente de la fe religiosa, pero no a todos les es dado beber de ella" (7:143). ("Many assuage the thirst for eternal life, above all the simple folk, in the fountain of religious faith, but it is not given to everyone to drink from it.")

arrive by faith to all of the truth.") It is as though Unamuno has personalized Christ's admonition that he who would find his life must first lose it to reflect the centrality of the intellect which must be surrendered in order to find life. In order to arrive at truth and live it, it is the intellect that must humble itself. A truly humble person is one who will humble his reasoning (8:810).

Part of humility is repentance. Unamuno uses the example of the thief who was crucified with Jesus to underscore the role of repentance in humility and his act of faith—asking to be remembered when Christ came into paradise. Unamuno asks, "Why was the thief saved?" Because in humility he saw his need and confessed it before God. In so doing the thief recognizes that Christ is divine, and he is not.

Unamuno knows what his own impediment to faith is. The opposite of humility is pride, and that is something Unamuno battles constantly. "Tengo que vencer ese oculto orgullo, esa costante rebusca de mí mismo, ese íntimo y callado endiosamiento, ese querer labrar mi propia estatua y deleitarme en mi idea de mí mismo, ese empeñarme en trabajar para la posteridad, esa necia vanidad de creerme de otra especie" (8:847). ("I have to defeat this hidden pride, this constant searching of myself, this intimate and quiet deification, this wanting to build my own statue and enjoy in myself the idea of myself, this striving to work for posterity, this foolish vanity of believing that I am of another species.") Unamuno's pride in his intellect and his reason are a stumbling block to faith. At one point he says that all of his intellectualizing has been transformed by a "new light". But he worries that he will be put to the ultimate test, "Tendré que sacrificar mi razón al cabo? Esto sería horrible" (8:843). ("Will I have to sacrifice my reason at the end? That would be horrible.") At this moment his desire for faith overcomes his reason. Immediately after the above he adds, "Pero hágase, Señor, tu voluntad y no la mía. Si la razón me daña, quítame la razón y dame paz y salud, aunque sea en la imbecilidad" (8:843). ("But Lord, do your will and not mine. If reason hurts me, take reason from me and give me peace and health, even if it be in idiocy.")

Unamuno worries about his inability to repent or confess. As noted in chapter 2, he says that his spiritual crisis cost him tears of anguish but not repentance. He wants to act in love, but he says there is nothing but concepts in his spirit and he cannot cry (8:784). He wants to be able to cry. He says that he resists receiving the kingdom of God as a child and resists confession (8:806). He is quite happy to reveal his state to anyone, but not to confess the way the church demands of him (8:811). He says that if he could ever find a saint, maybe he would submit to him, but how would he know that the person was a saint? (8:843). Unamuno is unable to repent of anything. "No logro llegar a contrición alguna, solo fríamente siento la atrición. Estoy lleno de mí mismo y mi ambición me espanta" (8:836). ("I cannnot come to the point of contrition, only coldly feeling the fear of the punishment of God. I am full of myself and my ambition frightens me.")

Unamuno questions the source of his own need for life to continue after death. He sees that he has put himself at the center of the universe, and if he dies, as he has vainly thought, so also the rest of the world dies (8:791). To push back from the terror of such an occurrence, he has sought God, but he wonders about his motivations. "Después de todo es poco pura esta costante preocupación mía por mi propio fin y destino. Es tal vez una forma aguda de egotismo. En vez de buscarme en Dios, busco a Dios en mí" (8:835). ("After all, it is not very pure this constant preoccupation of mine for my own end and destiny. It is perhaps a sharp form of egoism. Instead of looking for myself in God, I look for God in me.")

Near the end of the *Diario*, in the "Cuaderno Cuarto," he agonizes over comparing himself to the Biblical Ananias and Sapphira. They lied to the Apostle Peter about the price of the land which they sold, keeping back part of the money for themselves. Peter said that they had not lied to him but to God, and they paid for their misrepresentation of the truth in death. Unamuno asks himself why he gives part of himself to faith and reserves a part to himself, sometimes going ahead with the ritual but not with pure intentions, and he wonders if he isn't also lying to God as Ananias and Sapphira did (8:854).

Unamuno sees intellectualism as a terrible disease and those who suffer from the disease are unaware of it, just as those who are mad do not recognize their madness (8:811). He says that the pursuit of knowledge through intellectualism only leads to a dryness of spirit, which he reveals as his own at various points in the *Diario* (8:798, 803, 811, 825). It is as though his intellectual self will not allow him to embrace seriously anything beyond the verifiable as a remedy, a consolation for his tortured anxieties. The result is a hollowness and dryness of spirit.

But Unamuno's tendency is to fall into intellectualism over and over again (8:829). He wonders whether there are two "yos," two I's, that are warring within him, one who writes from his heart and another who rebels against precisely what he has written (8:843). He also knows that when he falls back into reason, he is often worrying about what others may think of him as the news of his "change" has circulated among the literati (8:816). He says that he does not want to be a slave to the image that the rest have of him. They can't possibly understand the call that God has put on his life. He wants the freedom to believe. "¡Libertad, Señor, libertad! Que viva en ti y no en cabezas que se reducirán a polvo," (8:822).("Freedom, Lord, Freedom! That I may live in you and not in heads that will be reduced to dust.")

So within the pages of the *Diario* we find moments of faith and moments of rebellion. Since there is a constant vacillation between the two, what can we conclude? We have already seen in chapter 2 that Unamuno said he had not returned to the congregation of the faithful the Easter after his time of spiritual crisis in March of 1897. We have later correspondence in which Unamuno characterized his attempt to restore the faith of his childhood as "false."[10] But there is enough evidence in the *Diario* itself to show that Unamuno was simply unable to embrace a simple, humble faith. The passages of rebellion overshadow the pleas for faith. Take, for example, "Es inútil que intente engañarme y que me obstine en vivir en ilusiones y alimentarme de ellas. Necesito realidades" (8:836).[11] ("It is useless to try to deceive myself and persist in living in illusions and nurturing myself from them. I need realities.") Unamuno asks for a sign even though he knows that he is precisely the sort of person to whom God does not give signs, because of his pride (8:873). He also knows that even if he were given a sign, he would not use it for its intent. "Pido una señal, una sola señal evidente, y preveo que si la obtuviera me metería a analizarla y aquilatarla" (8:827). ("I ask for a sign, just one evident sign, and I can foresee that if I were to obtain it, I would set myself to analyzing it and evaluating it.")

Even here in the *Diario*, long before the theory would be specifically defended in *Del sentimiento trágico,* we see the elevation of the struggle above finding resolution to it. "Así no se puede vivir, me digo. Pero así debo vivir, luchando con estas tentaciones, haciéndome a la muerte. ¿Quién sino Dios mismo me ha movido a que le busque? Me he burlado mucho de la duda; hoy vivo en dudas" (8:827). ("I tell myself, one can't live like that. But that is the way I should live, struggling with these temptations to my death. Who but God himself has motivated me to search for him? I have made a lot of fun of doubt; today I live in doubt.") God might have moved

10. Sánchez Barbudo, *Estudios de Unamuno y Machado*, 226, quotes Unamuno in a letter to Clarín of May 5, 1900 in which he characterizes his attempt to regain his childhood faith as "falso."

11. Malvido Miguel, *Unamuno a la busca*, 150, claims that Unamuno's inability to believe is clearly influenced by the positivism found in the scientific method.

Unamuno to seek him, but Unamuno will live with his doubts throughout his life. Fernández González concludes from the *Diario* that no one who has the security of faith would make such a problem of life after death. "Nadie que posea la seguridad que da la fe y aliente en la esperanza puede hacer un problema agónico del sobrevivir. Pero quien se alimenta de dudas y se plantea rigurosamente el problema del más allá vive en perpetua tensión."[12] ("No one who possesses the security of faith and who feeds on hope can make surviving an anguishing problem. The person who feeds himself with doubt and rigorously sets forth the problem of the great beyond lives in perpetual tension.")

Without a sign, without the peace that would come with traditional Christian faith, Unamuno outlines in the *Diario* the doctrine of *querer creer* (to want to believe) as his answer to the question of faith. Though calling it a doctrine would not please Unamuno, he held to his version of belief as tenaciously as anyone. The doctrine would be elucidated and defended in *Del sentimiento trágico,* but we see its beginnings in the *Diario.* Unamuno questions whether he should take communion with the congregation when he does not believe in the sacrament. It is an act of obedience, he thinks, but the humility with which one should obey should not just be a surrendering of one's will to do the act but also a surrendering of the mind to believe. He concludes, "No debo obedecer la ley hasta creer en ella como el pueblo, es una comunión de mentira" (8:806). ("I shouldn't obey the law until I believe in it as the people do; it is a communion of a lie.") Then, as if to explain himself further and perhaps to excuse himself, as well, he says, "Más que creer, quiero creer" (8:806). ("More than believing, I want to believe.") This is an important step in understanding the later, more specific insistence on the two sides, reason and faith, being maintained in tension. Unamuno does not want to give up his reason and his right to doubt, but he also will defend the demands of the heart by insisting that he wants to believe.[13]

Although he puts it in the form of a question, Unamuno would like to believe that whoever wants to believe already has some form of faith. "El querer creer, ¿no es principio de creer? El que desea fe y la pide, ¿no es que la tiene ya, aunque no lo sepa?" (8:827). ("Wanting to believe. Is that not the beginning of belief? He who wants faith asks for it, doesn't he

12. Fernández González, "Nueva lectura del *Diario íntimo,*" 375.

13. Zubizarreta, *Unamuno y su "nívola,"* 281, claims that throughout his life and even minutes before his death that Unamuno remained at the threshold of faith, holding on to the doctrine of wanting to believe over faith.

already have it, although he doesn't know it?") Having a faith that is hidden or unknown to the person seems somehow more acceptable to Unamuno. How does wanting to believe produce faith? Unamuno here gives a practical approach, and though he seemed to take it on for himself during the period in which the *Diario* was written, its results are questionable in his case. "¿Quieres creer? Pues imita desde luego esa vida y llegarás a creer. Condúcete como si creyeras y acabarás creyendo" (8:840). ("Do you want to believe? Then imitate that life and you will come to believe. Conduct yourself as though you believed and you will end up believing.")

By the time Unamuno writes *Del sentimiento trágico*, there is no more questioning about *querer creer*; rather, wanting to believe as the essence of faith is set forth as dogma. In "En el fondo del abismo" ("In the Depths of the Abyss"), Unamuno says of faith, "ésta no es en su esencia, sino cosa de voluntad, no de razón, como creer es querer creer, y creer en Dios ante todo y sobre todo es querer que le haya" (7:177). ("This [faith] is not in its essence anything but a matter of the will, not of reason, as to believe is to want to believe and to believe in God above all and over all is to want for him to exist.") To the ordinary person, Unamuno's claim that belief in God is the same as merely wanting him to exist may sound like wish fulfillment, and it may be that Unamuno expressed himself in such a way as to give that impression on purpose to shock the reader into paying attention to what he had to say. However, what Unamuno has in mind has a solid philosophical basis, and though he surely believed in the principle of *querer creer* before he read William James, he found in James a credible spokesperson for his point of view.[14]

Thomas Franz points out that, "Unamuno cited James with a certain stubborn irregularity from 1896 to 1936."[15] However, Franz agrees with Luis Farré that, "El norteamericano penetra en su ánimo de una manera más sutil e intelectual [que Kierkegaard]. Le proporciona argumentos y explicaciones para una posición que adoptara aun antes de conocerlo"[16] (110). ("The North American penetrates more subtly and intellectually

14. In *Agonía del cristianismo* Unamuno explicitly talks about James and his essay on "The Will to Believe." There Unamuno makes the point that the Spanish word for will, *voluntad*, has no root in the colloquial language. The Latin root *volere* or *velle* that would be *vouloir* in French is *querer* in Spanish. So his designation of *querer creer* is the equivalent of "the will to believe." He does not want *ganas* to be confused with *querer*. The point is that *ganas* has more to do with desire and appetite than with the will.

15. Franz, "*Niebla* and the Varieties of Religious Experience," 104.

16. Farré, *Unamuno, William James y Kierkegaard*, 110.

into his spirit [than does Kierkegaard]. He supplies him with arguments and explanations for a position that he might have adopted before being acquainted with him.") In James's "The Will to Believe," Unamuno found a very carefully argued justification for allowing one's will and one's passions to affect one's beliefs. James argues that religious belief is at least possible, even though it cannot be demonstrated "rationally." He presents, "a defense of our right to adopt a believing attitude in religious matters, in spite of the fact that our merely logical intellect may not have been coerced."[17]

Though admittedly a very rough summary, it would be well to review James's line of reasoning here. James delivered his now famous "The Will to Believe" lecture as an address to the Philosophical Clubs of Yale and Brown Universities, and it was first published in the *New World* in 1896.[18] He was trained in science and respected the objectivity of science, but he felt as though scientists were not justified in requiring the kind of objective evidence they worked for daily to answer metaphysical questions where no objective evidence was obtainable. He believed that scientists were also blind to how their "faith" in materialism affected realms where beliefs were not appropriately decided by objective facts. James defines a decision between two hypotheses as a genuine option when it is a living, forced and momentous option. To be a living option, both hypotheses must be psychologically believable, views a person could accept and act on. A forced option is one where a decision cannot be avoided; failing to choose is equivalent to choosing one of the options. To be a momentous option the stakes must be very high; we are convinced that our lives will be wholly different as a result of the decision.

James holds various presuppositions, some perhaps more questionable than others, particularly today. He assumes that all will agree that there is something called Truth and that we are made so as to want to obtain the truth. He says that he is an empiricist, not an absolutist. He believes in objective truth but does not claim that he would know beyond a shadow of a doubt that he has obtained it. Since we are such fallible creatures, likely to make mistakes no matter what, he does not think we should have an exaggerated fear of being wrong.

There are two things we want as believers: to find truth and to avoid error. The person who says we must not believe when the evidence is inconclusive is saying that it is more important to avoid error than to find truth.

17. James, "Will to Believe," 13.
18. Ibid.

But such a choice is itself the expression of a passionate preference, an inordinate desire to avoid error. It is therefore irrational for such a rationalist to argue that our desires should not affect our beliefs, for his own recommended policy about beliefs is itself an expression of his desire: "Our passional nature not only lawfully may, but must, decide an option between propositions, whenever it is a genuine option that cannot by its nature be decided on intellectual grounds; for to say, under such circumstances, 'Do not decide, but leave the question open,' is itself a passional decision—just like deciding yes or no—and is attended with the same risk of losing the truth."[19]

James says that moral beliefs involve forced options. They are ones that must be made whether there is objective evidence or not. Science can tell us objective facts, but a moral question is one that asks if something is good, and that is entirely outside of the kind of truth that science can verify. And the basis on which we make moral decisions is often decided by our will, what we want to be the case. He gives the example of social relationships such as those between friends or lovers. In order to find out if friendship or love exists between the persons, the person must act as though those conditions apply before friendship and love can be proved to be present. Believing that they exist is required before they can exist, and what's more, the belief brings the friendship or the love into existence. "The desire for a certain kind of truth here brings about that special truth's existence."[20]

The same logic applies to the religious hypothesis. If there is a Thou to the universe that we normally designate as God, then one must make an active, believing step in God's direction before one can come into relationship with the Thou. We would never have evidence of God existing without that step toward the Thou. James states that generically it can be said that all religions affirm essentially the same two things: "The best things are the more eternal things," and "The second affirmation of religion is that we are better off even now if we believe her [religion's] first affirmation to be true."[21] James recognizes that the religious hypothesis must be a living option for us, even if it is also momentous and forced. For him, skepticism is not an option. "Skepticism, then, is not avoidance of option; it is option for a certain particular kind of risk. *Better risk loss of truth than chance of error*—that is your faith vetoer's exact position."[22] James believes that the will has a role to play in the deciding on the religious hypothesis and that

19. Ibid., 20.
20. Ibid., 28.
21. Ibid., 29–30.
22. Ibid., 30.

the actions that result from believing the religious hypothesis matter. "If the action required or inspired by the religious hypothesis is in no way different from that dictated by the naturalistic hypothesis, then religious faith is a pure superfluity."[23] For James, faith matters as it determines our actions.

Let us see how James helps Unamuno with the problem of immortality. Once again, Unamuno believes that the heart demands belief that there be life after death but the head, reason, tells him that that is impossible. The desire to live beyond death is so strong that multiple means of obtaining immortality are developed, those of one's children living out your legacy, your literary children provoking the reader to recreate you and your fame, your name being sustained throughout history. Though attempts to achieve immortality through children, literature and fame are powerfully seductive, the only sure way for there to be immortality is for there to be a God who can guarantee that immortality. We have seen Unamuno's struggle to regain the faith of his childhood, a struggle between the intellect and faith. It seems as though the intellect wins. Unamuno rejects the traditional proofs for God's existence and finds them worthless because God cannot be rationalized. "Las supuestas pruebas clásicas de la existencia de Dios refiérense todas a este Dios-Idea, a este Dios lógico, al Dios por remoción, y de aquí que en rigor no prueben nada, es decir, no prueban más que la existencia de esa idea de Dios" (7:204). ("The supposed classical proofs for God's existence all refer to this God-Idea, to this logical God, to the God of abstraction, and from there they really prove nothing, that is to say, they don't prove more than the existence of that idea of God.") Since Unamuno recognizes that God cannot be proved rationally, he must have some other impetus, some other ground to believe if there is to be a divine guarantor of his immortality. James helps to provide that ground.

When Unamuno says, "La razón nos aparta más bien de Él [Dios]. No es posible conocerle para luego amarle; hay que empezar por amarle, por anhelarle, por tener hambre de Él, antes de conocerle" (7:208). ("Reason separates us from God. It is not possible to know him in order that we might afterwards love him; one must begin by loving him, by longing for him, by hungering for him, before knowing him,") we hear an echo of James's example of the first step toward the Thou making a relationship with God possible. Without the longing and the action toward the Thou, the relationship would not come into being. Unamuno describes his own experience in turning from reason and making that step in the following passage:

23. Ibid., 32.

> Mientras peregriné por los campos de la razón a busca de Dios, no pude encontrarle . . . y fue entonces, cuando erraba por los páramos del racionalismo, cuando me dije que no debemos buscar más consuelo que la verdad, llamando así a la razón, sin que por eso me consolara. Pero al ir hundiéndome en el escepticismo racional de una parte y en la desesperación sentimental de otra, se me encendió el hambre de Dios y el ahogo de espíritu me hizo sentir con su falta su realidad. Y quise que haya Dios, que exista Dios. Y Dios no existe, sino que más bien sobre-existe y está sustentando nuestra existencia, existiéndonos (7:209).

> (While I made my pilgrimage through the fields of reason in search of God, I could not find him . . . and it was then, when I wandered through the wastelands of rationalism, when I told myself, we should not seek any other consolation other than the truth, meaning thereby, reason, and yet for all that I was not comforted. But upon sinking into rational skepticism on the one hand and into heart's despair on the other, the hunger for God was awakened in me and the sense of drowning of the spirit made me feel His reality for want of him. And I wanted that there be a God, for God to exist. And God does not exist, but rather super-exists, and He is sustaining our existence, existing us.)

Admittedly, Unamuno's insistence that God doesn't exist but rather that he "super exists" muddies the water. However, the movement from the sterile confines of skepticism, caused by the emphasis on truth only being achieved through reason, to embracing the "sentimental" or "heart's" desire that there be a God is what James calls for. This is James's passional nature being allowed to hold sway in the matter of a deciding between hypotheses when there is a genuine option.

Unamuno needs God to give meaning to his life and to guarantee his survival after death, but he dodges the question of whether that God exists outside of his need for him. "Esa persona eterna y eternizadora que da sentido . . . al Universo, ¿es algo sustancial fuera de nuestra conciencia, fuera de nuestro anhelo? He aquí algo insoluble, y vale más que así lo sea. Bástele a la razón el no poder probar la imposibilidad de su existencia" (7:218–19).[24] (That eternal and eternalizing person who gives meaning . . .to the Universe, is he something substantial, outside of our consciousness, outside of our longing? Here is something unsolvable, and it is better that it be

---

24. Malvido Miguel, *Unamuno a la busca de la inmortalidad*, 150, criticizes Unamuno's epistemology when he insists that the only way of knowing is the positivistic supposedly 'scientific' evidence gained by observation.

that way. Let it be enough for reason that it cannot prove the impossibility of his existence.") So Unamuno recognizes with James that reason cannot disprove the objective existence of God outside of our consciousness or independent of our desire that he exist. That is important for maintaining belief as a living option. For Unamuno, *querer creer*, to want to believe, is enough. Unamuno believes that *querer creer* is enough because he believes that his actions can be conformed to the belief that God exists, whether there be any God that exists apart from his desire that he exist (7:219).[25]

Although Unamuno has used James's justification for religious belief on the basis of the will, it is not clear how far the two thinkers agree. James maintains that religious belief is possible through means other than reason, though his sense of religious belief is vague and most certainly is not specifically a justification of traditional Christianity.[26] But he believes, at least at some moments, that the faith that one comes to has as its object a reality that transcends the individual. The person has been brought to faith in something "more" than the natural world. This something "more" towards whom the person has stepped seems to be a real Thou, even if it is posited partly as a result of our own need to believe.[27] Unamuno, however, wants to reserve judgment on the question of God's existence. Is there a part of James's justification for religious belief that Unamuno has left to one side?

You will recall that James began his explanation of his justification for religious belief on the basis of will with a very careful definition of what a genuine option entails before claiming, "Our passional nature not only lawfully may, but must, decide an option between propositions whenever it is a genuine option that cannot by its nature be decided on intellectual grounds."[28] A genuine option must be one that is living, forced and momentous. The problem for Unamuno is that belief in God's existence is ultimately not fully a live option. James explains that "deadness and liveness in an hypothesis are not intrinsic properties, but relations to the individual

---

25. Farré, *Unamuno, William James y Kierkegaard*, 89, believes that James and Unamuno are both persons who merely "want to believe," even though James puts forward the argument that passional attitudes must be taken into consideration when deciding questions that are metaphysical in nature.

26. In *Varieties of Religious Experience* James calls the particular theology of Christianity an "over belief" and says explicitly that he is not arguing for it. "That would be unfair to other religions," 501.

27. For a discussion of the meaning of a something "more" and its truth, see ibid., 500–504.

28. James, "Will to Believe," 20.

thinker. They are measured by his willingness to act. The maximum of liveness in an hypothesis means willingness to act irrevocably. Practically, that means belief."[29] Although belief is dependent on the ability to act, it still has an intellectual component that Unamuno seems unwilling to concede. For James, a live option is one that has intellectual credibility on both sides of the equation. Then, he allows the heart and the will to decide between the two. For Unamuno reason is entirely on the side of unbelief. There is no rational credibility for belief. To believe is to give up rationality altogether.

Unamuno is unwilling to act irrevocably and believe in the hypothesis that God exists because he is psychologically unable to give up the intellectual doubts that are at the core of his world view. James certainly shares some of those doubts; perhaps a full-fledged theistic belief is not a live option for him either. But he seems, again at least at some moments, to have overcome his doubts to attain a vague belief in some kind of personal reality beyond the physical universe.[30]

Though Unamuno says that the question of our life beyond this one is the only question that matters, he is unwilling to make the leap to believe in the God who would guarantee his immortality. He puts forward the doctrine of *querer creer* to satisfy his heart, but his head maintains the passionate uncertainty of intellectual doubt, and he says that he will live from the tension between the two. From 1902 on, it was clear that Unamuno would not attempt any compromise between faith and reason. In a letter to Santiago Valentí on March 11 of 1902 Unamuno outlines the thesis for what would later be *Del sentimiento trágico de la vida*: "La tesis central es la irreductibilidad de la ciencia y la religión, aquélla es anti-religiosa, ésta anticientífica, y sin embargo, la necesidad de aceptar ambas y de aceptarlas como irreductibles."[31] ("The central thesis is the irreducibility of science and religion; the former is anti-religious and the latter is anti-scientific, but there is a need to accept them both and to accept them as irreducible.") Later, in *Del sentimiento trágico*, Unamuno articulates the essence of that irreducibility as war between two equal and opposing forces that become the center of his spiritual life (7:172). As we have seen, what results is a life of contradiction from which Unamuno does not shrink. "Es la contradicción

29. Ibid., 14.

30. See the conclusion of *Varieties of Religious Experience*, particularly 505 and following.

31. Unamuno, quoted in Malvido Miguel, *Unamuno a la busca de la inmortalidad*, 250.

íntima precisamente lo que unifica mi vida y le da razón práctica de ser. O más bien es el conflicto mismo, es la misma apasionada incertidumbre lo que unifica mi acción y me hace vivir y obrar" (7:262). ("It is precisely this inner contradiction that unifies my life and gives it its practical reason for being. It is the conflict itself, it is this self-same passionate uncertainty, that unifies my action and makes me live and work.")

We began this chapter with a question about Unamuno's obsession for his own life to be preserved after death. Was it at bottom just narcissism or did it lead to a foundation on which one could base religious belief in a God who would be the guarantor of our immortality? There is abundant evidence from the *Diario* that Unamuno himself worried about his obsession being driven by egoism in the extreme. Throughout his life Unamuno's need for his work to be well received and for his fame to be broad was not hidden.[32] Regardless of how egoistic Unamuno may have been, no serious reader can deny that his concern is a universal human preoccupation. If we believe that it is natural for humans to think about and desire life after death, then Unamuno's concern, while it may be expressed more strongly than it is for most people, still expresses a universal human need.

It may be, as Sánchez Barbudo contends, that after the spiritual crisis of 1897 and his subsequent realization that he could not regain the faith of his childhood, Unamuno sought to assure his immortality through his literary production.[33] But Unamuno's faith, his *querer creer,* was also at work in tension with his rational self that set about leaving his mark on history in ways other than the supernatural. If Unamuno is to be known as a man of contradiction, as he wanted to be, then the faith part of the reason/faith dichotomy must be just as alive and well as the intellectual, doubting part. Unamuno's definition of faith is *querer creer,* even if equating wanting to believe with faith does not fully square with traditional Christianity.

How is all this helpful to the contemporary fellow traveler who is wrestling with the end of life? Unamuno is almost never gentle in his pronouncements, but he respects his reader and shares his struggle with the expectation that the truth both he and his reader are after is larger than either of them. As he explains in the *Diario*, he writes so that his reader

32. Malvido Miguel, *Unamuno a la busca de inmortalidad* , 273, records the remarkable collection of Unamuno's letters of his own commentary on the reception of *Del sentimiento trágico.* Unamuno notes each review and eagerly tells his correspondents about new editions of his "obra capital" as they come out. As late as 1935 he was still counting the translations, by then six.

33. Sánchez Barbudo, "Una experiencia decisiva: la crisis de 1897," 102.

may decide for himself or herself about these ultimate questions: "Expón, con sinceridad y sencillez tu sentir y deja que la verdad obre por sí sobre la mente de tu hermano; que le gane ella y no que le sojuzgues tú. La verdad que profieras no es tuya, está sobre ti y se basta a sí misma" (7:791). ("Expound your meaning with sincerity and simplicity and allow the truth to work by itself on the mind of your brother; let the truth win over that mind and do not conquer it yourself. The truth that you offer is not yours, it is bigger than you and it is enough in itself.")

Like James, Unamuno puts forward a forceful ground for belief in allowing one's passional nature to decide metaphysical questions for those who seek life-giving truth through practical reason. For both thinkers, the "will to believe" is the justifiable key to faith. However, Unamuno ultimately answers the question of immortality from opposing views, faith and reason, without compromise, holding the two in tension. The next chapter will more fully explain the relationship between faith and reason, underscoring the central role of doubt in maintaining the necessary tension for Unamuno.

5

Unamuno, Kierkegaard, and Pascal on the Role of Doubt in Faith

UNAMUNO SEES KIERKEGAARD AND Pascal as writers who share his passion and his agonic spirit. As was noted in the Introduction, in *La agonía del cristianismo,* Unamuno so identifies with both Pascal and Kierkegaard that he says that he has lived in their time and in their world (7:314). Unamuno believes that they share his concern about the ultimate question of immortality, and it is true that Pascal is just as passionate as Unamuno in his concern for life after death. Unamuno quotes Pascal when discussing indifference to the question of immortality: "Como Pascal, no comprendo al que asegura no dársele un ardite de este asunto, y ese abandono en cosa 'en que se trata de ellos mismos, de su eternidad, de su todo, me irrita más que me enternece, me asombra y me espanta'" (7:133). ("Like Pascal, I cannot understand the person who self-assuredly says that this matter doesn't concern him a bit, this abandonment of something, 'that is about the essence of themselves, of their eternity, of their all, irritates me more than it moves me to pity; it surprises me and frightens me.'") With Pascal, Unamuno calls those who don't care about their eternal fate "monsters."

Kierkegaard shares Unamuno's concern about existence and relates all of our present existence to our eternal happiness. Unamuno calls Kierkegaard his brother and uses a long quote from *Concluding Unscientific Postscript* to shore up his argument that abstract thought about immortality kills the individual's sense of existence because what remains is theoretical. "El pensador abstracto no le sirve a mi inmortalidad sino para matarme en cuanto individuo singularmente existente" (7:174).

("The abstract thinker does not serve me or my immortality, but rather he kills me as an individual singularly existing.")

So Pascal and Kierkegaard, like Unamuno, have a passionate concern for life after death. Whether they fully share Unamuno's perspective remains to be seen, but there is at least a common conviction that this issue involves some degree of uncertainty. This concern for life after death also is linked to belief in God, since in order to believe that there is life after this one, there needs to be a God who is the guarantor of that life. Faith in God makes possible a faith that this life will not be the end of me, my thinking, willing being.

Though Unamuno desperately wants to believe in a God who would be the guarantor of life after death, doubt regularly gets in the way of that faith. Unamuno clearly felt drawn to Pascal and Kierkegaard because of their shared passions. However, though each deals extensively with the possibility of faith as an answer to the question of immortality, Pascal and Kierkegaard do not wholly share Unamuno's embrace of doubt. In order to understand the differences, it will be helpful to explore how each thinker relates faith and reason and how each reacts to what I will call the hiddenness of God. Ultimately, it is Unamuno's view of reason that is the source of his inability to make the leap of faith that Kierkegaard and Pascal make. I will first outline what Unamuno means by doubt and then explain his insistence on the foundational nature of doubt for understanding existence and living it.

Since reason tells us objectively that our lives end, and our heart's desire is for that not to be the case, Unamuno finds hope in a life of doubt. For him, doubt is not just religious doubt; it extends to doubt of what we learn from the "head": doubt about reason and science. His chapter, "En el fondo del absimo" ("In the Depths of the Abyss"), in *Del sentimiento trágico de la vida* maintains that skepticism about the possibility of any life after this one must face the force of our will to live, and recommends that the two— skepticism about life after death and a fervent desire for life after death— "embrace like brothers" (7:172). The resulting skepticism and uncertainty then form the basis of the hope that counters the desperation of the heart. Doubt brings hope because reason is not allowed the last word about our final end. However, the same doubt is applied to our heart's desire to live on after death. "La paz entre estas dos potencias se hace imposible, y hay que vivir de su Guerra. Y hacer de ésta, de la guerra misma, condición de nuestra vida espiritual" (7:172). ("Peace between these two powers is impossible, and one must live from their war. And one must make of that war, of war itself, the condition of our spiritual life.")

Unamuno wants nothing to do with Cartesian doubt. Rene Descartes' (1596–1650) attempt to know by doubting everything seems to Unamuno to be a non-starter. He makes fun of such comic, methodological doubt and calls it "philosophical doubt of the stove" (7:173). Rather, what Unamuno has in mind is passionate doubt, "Es el eterno conflicto entre la razón y el sentimiento, la ciencia y la vida, la lógica y la biótica" (7:173). ("It is the eternal conflict between reason and feeling, between knowledge and life, between logic and the biotic.") One must doubt reason because the longing for immortality lies outside of rationality. However, any faith that would allow you to believe in immortality needs the challenge of reason. Unamuno insists that faith and reason need each other but that mutual need is expressed in tension, not in reconciliation or synthesis. "Razón y fe son dos enemigos que no pueden sostenerse el uno sin el otro. Lo irracional pide ser racionalizado, y la razón sólo puede operar sobre lo irracional. Tienen que apoyarse uno en otro y asociarse. Pero asociarse en lucha, ya que la lucha es un modo de asociación" (7:175). ("Faith and reason are two enemies that cannot be sustained the one without the other. That which is irrational demands to be rationalized, and reason can only operate on what is irrational. They have to support each other and associate with each other. But to associate in struggle since struggle is a means of association.)

Unamuno applies doubt equally to both faith and reason, but he describes the two differently. Rationalism or reason is equated with intelligence and the instinct of knowing. Vitalism or faith is equated with the will and the instinct of survival. The only thing that is sure is that absolute doubt (skepticism) and absolute certainty are both excluded. Unamuno states that a total skeptic's life is not possible because then a person would be required to doubt his very existence. Likewise certainty, either that life ends with death or that there is a future existence after death, is unbelievable as well because there is a still small voice within us that questions both. Unamuno wants to keep both voices talking to each other; sometimes, in his works, it seems like they scream at each other. He says, "Por mi parte no quiero poner paz entre mi corazón y mi cabeza, entre me fe y mi razón; quiero más bien que se peleen entre sí" (7:180). ("For my part, I do not want peace between my heart and my head, between my faith and my reason; rather, I want for them to fight each other.")

What can Unamuno mean when he says that doubt is just as important on the faith side of the equation as on the side of reason? He refers in many places, but particularly in *Del sentimiento trágico,* to the story in Mark's gospel about the father who brought his son who was possessed by demons to be cured by Jesus. The disciples had tried to exorcise the demons and had been unsuccessful. The father was desperate. In his request to Jesus the father revealed his less than robust faith. He put the request in terms of "if you are able to do anything, have pity on us and help us." Jesus called him on his vacillation and said, "'If you are able!—All things can be done for the one who believes." To which the father replied, "I believe; help my unbelief!"[1] Unamuno says that the father demonstrated faith based on incertitude. It is the faith that Sancho Panza had in Don Quixote and the faith of Don Quixote himself. "Nuestro Señor Don Quijote es el ejemplar vitalista cuya fe se basa en incertidumbre y Sancho lo es del racionalista que duda de su razón" (7:180–81). ("Our lord Don Quixote is the prototype of the vitalist whose faith is based on uncertainty and Sancho is the prototype of the rationalist who doubts his own reason.") Unamuno says that the father who wanted his son to be healed demonstrated the faith of *querer creer,* to want to believe, which is a matter of the will, not of reason, as we saw in chapter 4.

The negative contrast is with the faith of *el carbonero,* the coal delivery man, who never questions his faith. Unamuno mentions this character in multiple places. This is a person who unthinkingly accepts faith, and when anyone asks a troubling question *el carbonero,* along with many who are taught the Catholic catechism, say, "Do not ask me the reason of that, for I am ignorant; Holy Mother church possesses doctors who will know how to answer you." Unamuno sees this as an evasion, rather than as proper humility, and he would not tolerate it. He calls the coal delivery man's faith an absurd faith, but his criticism is not limited to the humble, uneducated *carbonero.* Unamuno also excoriates the incredulity of the intellectual who is equally unable to test his assumptions. He equates the absurd faith of the coal delivery man with the absurd incredulity of the intellectual and considers them both stupid (7:181). The certainty of *el carbonero* and the incredulous intellectual is the sort of certainty that is the basis for dogmatism against which Unamuno fought in all its forms for all of his life.

In *La agonía del crisianismo* the depth of the struggle and the darkness of the doubt seems to be starker. Here, too, Unamuno appeals to scripture, this time from Luke 12, where Jesus said that he did not come to bring peace, but rather a sword. Jesus pointed to the fact that to follow him may require normal relationships to be broken, those of a son to his father, a daughter to her mother and even a daughter-in-law to her mother-in-law.

1. Mark 9:23–24 (NRSV).

What Unamuno hears from the scripture is that you can't have peace without war and visa versa. Conflict will always be present. He admits that there may be many other passages about the peace that the Gospel is to bring, but he claims to be in the company of St. Paul, St. Augustine and Pascal in his emphasis on the polemical nature of Christianity.

For Unamuno, the center of the polemical nature of Christianity is doubt. "El modo de vivir, de luchar, de luchar por la vida y vivir de la lucha, de la fe, es dudar" (7:311). ("The way to live, to struggle, to struggle for life and to live from the struggle, to live from faith, is to doubt.") This is so because even Christ doubted as he said on the cross, "My God, my God, why have you forsaken me?"[2] Unamuno underscores that the depiction of Christ before which the Spanish believer worships is the agonizing Christ, not the Christ at peace in death, or one might add, the Christ of the resurrection. It is the Christ on the cross who calls out to question God in his own pain and struggle. Always the linguist, Unamuno explains the root of the verb *dudar* from the Latin *dubitare* which makes clearer the root, *duo* or two. For Unamuno "the two" is the equivalent of struggle, and for him that must be the essence of existence. Unamuno summarizes by saying, "Afirmo, creo, como poeta, como creador, mirando al pasado, al recuerdo; niego, descreo, como razonador, como ciudadano, mirando al presente, y dudo. Lucho, agonizo como hombre, como cristiano, mirando al porvenir irrealizable a la eternidad" (7:311). ("I affirm, I believe as a poet, as a creator, looking to the past, to memory; I deny, I disbelieve as a rational being, as a citizen, looking at the present, and I doubt. I struggle, I agonize as a man, as a Christian, looking at the unrealizable future of eternity.") So the contrast is between the poet and creator part of him which affirms and believes and the rational part of him that denies, disbelieves and doubts. The part of him that struggles between the two he identifies as Christian, the one with which he tries to make sense of eternity. For Unamuno there is no part that can be left out.

I shall try to show that Unamuno's picture of faith differs significantly from the views of Pascal and Kierkegaard, even though he is correct to see that they share his distaste for dogmatism and his recognition of the human condition as one that includes some degree of uncertainty. The differences between Unamuno and the two Christian thinkers center on their views about doubt. To begin we can note Pascal is just as hard on Descartes as Unamuno. It is not Descartes' sort of doubt that these three authors are interested in. In *Pensée* 84 Pascal says, "Descartes. In general one must say:

2. Mark 15:34 (NRSV).

Pointless, uncertain, and arduous. Even if it were true we do not think that the whole of philosophy would be worth an hour's effort."[3] Kierkegaard is kinder to Descartes but very critical of the Hegelian view that philosophy begins with a kind of doubt—an exhaustive critical reflection.[4] In *Philosophical Fragments* the author compares Hegelian doubt and Greek skepticism. He says, "We must not lay at his [the Greek's] door the stupid opinion [referring to the Hegelian] that one doubts by way of necessity, as well as the even more stupid opinion that, if that were the case, doubt could be terminated" (PF 82). Beginnning with doubt is dismissed as a viable method of doing philosophy.

Second, as already noted, there's the matter of dogmatism. All three authors bristle at the kind of certainty that gives rise to dogmatism. For Kierkegaard the dogmatist takes away the dialectical, which in this case means simply the ability to question. In *Concluding Unscientific Postscript* his pseudonym Climacus says, "Whether it is a word, a sentence, a book, a man, a society, whatever it is, as soon as it is supposed to be a boundary, so that the boundary itself is not dialectical, it is superstition and narrowmindedness. In a human being there is always a desire, at once comfortable and concerned, to have something really firm and fixed that can exclude the dialectical, but this is cowardliness and fraudulence toward the divine" (CUP: 35n). He says that even in revelation, where one would be claiming a fair amount of certainty if one believes that he has heard a message from God, there is still the possibility of the dialectical in the moment that the person appropriates the revelation.

Pascal has equally harsh things to say about the dogmatist and the skeptic[5]. He maintains that the person who says that he is the certain possessor of the truth is just as wrong as the skeptic who doubts everything. The key here is the misuse of reason. The dogmatist claims too much for reason and the skeptic not enough. Pascal says, "*Instinct, reason.* We have an incapacity for proving anything which no amount of dogmatism can

---

3. Pascal, *Pensées*, 84:52. This and all subsequent passages from Pascal will be noted throughout by first quoting the number of the fragment and then the page on which it can be found in the Krailsheimer translation.

4. See the somewhat surprising remarks about Descartes in *Fear and Trembling* where Descartes is praised as a thinker who "did what he said and said what he did" and who did not recommend doubt with respect to matters of faith (Kierkegaard, *Fear and Trembling, Repetition*, 6–7).

5. I am indebted to Peter Kreeft and his book *Christianity for Modern Pagans: Pascal's Pensees* for his insights into Pascal's work.

overcome. We have an idea of truth which no amount of skepticism can overcome."[6] This reflects the dual nature of humankind—that the human person is both wonderful and wretched—but recognition of that nature is impossible apart from help from God. For Pascal, human reason as it is used to justify certainty is bound to fail because of our fallen nature. Human reason is flawed by sin. Yes, there is a natural, created capacity to know something of the truth that is God-given, but only in faith can one overcome the flaw and be given the truth about one's own condition. Therefore Pascal says, "Know then, proud man, what a paradox you are to yourself. Be humble, impotent reason! Be silent, feeble nature! Learn that man infinitely transcends man, hear from your master your true condition, which is unknown to you. Listen to God."[7]

It is not surprising that Unamuno, Kierkegaard and Pascal share a dim view of the so-called proofs for God's existence, given their suspicion of claims to certainty, but their objections to the proofs differ. Unamuno says that he lost his faith while trying to rationalize it, as the classical proofs for God's existence attempt to do (7:204). His contention is with scholastic theology that he says created *cristianismo despotencializad* (emasculated Christianity), which took away the felt, loving God that guarantees immortality. For Unamuno, Thomistic proofs for the existence of God, though they attempt to use reason, actually make the faith "super-rational" when in fact it is "contra-rational" (7:155).

Unamuno also objects to having to swallow the whole of Catholic theology that has been developed over centuries by the same "doctors of the Church" (7:154). Unamuno does not think that the proofs work, and he resents having to believe that they do. He says that the Church considers the biggest sin that of heresy, of thinking for oneself, and that is what he declares that he will do. So, Unamuno's objections to the proofs for God's existence are rooted in the Church's assumption that reason does demonstrate the existence of God, and that the proofs are therefore compelling. The proofs demand that any reasonable person will agree that God exists. Unamuno considers himself a reasonable person and is not persuaded.

Certainly there are some similarities between this reaction on the part of Unamuno to rational apologetics and Kierkegaard's aversion to rational arguments for Christianity. C. Stephen Evans points out that there is evidence of Kierkegaard's resistance to apologetics in his signed works as well

6. Pascal, *Pensées*, 406:147.

7. Ibid., 131:65.

as his pseudonymous ones.[8] In *Works of Love* Kierkegaard states, "woe to the person who could make the miracle reasonable" (WL 200). Evans says that Kierkegaard, "rejects the idea of proving God's existence, not primarily because the proofs are bad, though he thinks they are less than conclusive, but because they make it appear that something (the existence of God) that should be certain for an individual is doubtful."[9] In *Concluding Unscientific Postcript* Johannes Climacus says that it is ridiculous to attempt to prove the existence of someone who is present to the exister, and it's actually an affront (CUP 545). In *Philosophical Fragments,* he makes fun of anyone who would attempt to prove God's existence saying, "Therefore, anyone who wants to demonstrate the existence of God . . . proves something else instead, at times something that perhaps did not even need demonstrating, and in any case never anything better. For the fool says in his heart that there is no God, but he who says in his heart or to others: Just wait a little and I shall demonstrate it—ah, what a rare wise man he is!" (PF 43).

In addition to Kierkegaard's objections to proofs of God existence are his objections to proofs of the truth of Christianity and the truth of the incarnation. Climacus speaks of the paradox, that God came to earth and became man, as the essence of Christianity. The human reaction to the paradox is either faith or offence. Climacus worries that an apologetic proof might make believing Christianity more palatable and take away the ability of the paradox to offend.[10] When the understanding meets the paradox and responds in faith, "the understanding surrenders itself and the paradox gives itself" (PF: 54). If reason insists upon understanding the paradox, then the result will be offense. Climacus' objection to apologetic proofs stems from his objection to anything that would lessen the need for faith. If reason alone can get the person to belief in God, what is the use of faith?

In agreement with Kierkegaard, Pascal insists that faith is God's doing and no amount of reason can get a person to believe that God exists. However, he has some appreciation for the place of proofs in the process toward faith. "Faith is different from proof. One is human and the other a gift from God . . . This is the faith that God himself puts into our hearts, often using proof as the instrument."[11] Pascal is not against using reason for good purpose. "Men despise religion, they hate it and are afraid it might be

8. C. S. Evans, "Apologetic Arguments in *Philosophical Fragments*," 133.

9. Ibid., "Can God Be Hidden and Evident?" 241.

10. Ibid., "Apologetic Arguments," 141.

11. Pascal, *Pensées*, 7:34.

true. To cure that we have to begin by showing that religion is not contrary to reason."[12] However, showing that religion is not contrary to reason is not the same as conclusive proof.

According to Pascal, one of the reasons that proofs for God's existence cannot be compelling is that there must be room for the freedom of will. The person must decide for himself or herself; God will not force himself on the person. He says, "The way of God, who disposes all things with gentleness, is to instill religion into our minds with reasoned arguments and into our hearts with grace, but attempting to instill it into hearts and minds with force and threats is to instill not religion but terror."[13] The way of God with us should help us understand how we also should behave—to allow freedom to choose for those whom we try to persuade of his existence. Further explaining, Pascal says, "If we submit everything to reason our religion will be left with nothing mysterious or supernatural. If we offend the principles of reason our religion will be absurd and ridiculous."[14] So Pascal sees an important role for reason. It is a necessary component of faith, but it is not sufficient. Kierkegaard would agree. Though many have characterized the Kierkegaardian "leap of faith" as being a leap into the absurd, this is an over simplification. For Kierkegaard the leap is a matter of choice. It will appear absurd to the person who lacks faith, but not so for the person of faith. Offense is not more rational than faith. Both are passionate responses to an encounter with the paradox.[15]

So far, we have looked mainly at areas where there is broad agreement between Unamuno, Pascal, and Kierkegaard, an agreement that makes understandable Unamuno's sense of spiritual kinship with these two thinkers. We have seen that none of the three thinkers bought into Cartesian doubt and all are wary of anyone who claims to have absolute certainty. Therefore they stand stridently against dogmatism of any kind. Their shared suspicion of proofs for God's existence is not a surprise, then, but the reasons for their rejection of the proofs begin to show some basic differences between Unamuno and the other two philosophers. For Kierkegaard and Pascal, those differences have as much to do with the limits of reason as they do with the appreciation of the work of providence in faith. Unamuno wants

12. Ibid., 12:34.

13. Ibid., 172:83

14. Ibid., 173:83.

15. See C. S. Evans, "Is Kierkegaard an Irrationalist?" particularly 129–30.

to keep doubt and faith in continual tension. Certainty, dogmatism and the proofs of God's existence are intellectual matters that all three authors address, but Kierkegaard and Pascal do not share Unamuno's angst about the inability to know conclusively. All three authors are persons who embrace the importance of the matters of the heart. However, Unamuno's embrace of the life of pain and conflict sounds a somewhat different note than can be found in Pascal and Kierkegaard.

In the section of *La agonía del cristianismo,* where Unamuno self identifies with Pascal and Kierkegaard, the Spanish philosopher claims that the doubt of which he speaks is agonic, polemic and Pascalian. Is he justified in such a claim? Already we have noted Pascal's disgust at the person who is indifferent to the question of immortality or the person who lives a life so engrossed in pleasure that he has not stopped to consider the importance of the matter. But is the search for an answer to the question of immortality as problematic for Pascal? It seems so in the following quote: "I condemn equally those who choose to praise man, those who choose to condemn him, and those who choose to divert themselves, and I can only approve of those who seek with groans."[16] Pascal is rejecting both the optimists and the pessimists about human nature and along with them those who avoid the difficulty by enjoying life and not thinking. He only endorses those who are searching for truth and admits that it is an agonizing process. However, unlike Unamuno, Pascal does not glorify the agonizing process itself; he holds out hope that one can overcome the agony.

To be sure, it seems like Pascal has experienced some of the same struggle that Unamuno displays when he says, "I look around in every direction and all I see is darkness. Nature has nothing to offer me that does not give rise to doubt and anxiety."[17] He goes on to say that Nature does not give conclusive evidence for or against the existence of God, though he would like for God to have displayed himself more clearly so that he should know the course he should take. He concludes this *Pensée* by saying, "Instead of that, in the state in which I am, not knowing what I am nor what I ought to do, I know neither my condition nor my duty. My whole heart strains to know what the true good is in order to pursue it: no price would be too high to pay for eternity."[18]

16. Pascal, *Pensées*, 405:146–47.

17. Ibid., 429:162.

18. Ibid., 429:163.

It is fair to say that Pascal experienced doubt and had great compassion for those who faced it daily, but to say that Pascal was caught up in a life-struggle like Unamuno's would not do justice to the rest of the *Pensées*. They reveal a Pascal who thought that if nature proved God then we would not have to seek him with our hearts. For Pascal there is a clear source of Truth and that is Christ, but finding his truth requires passionate searching that depends on the heart and on the will, not just the mind that might be persuaded by nature. Much later in the *Pensées* Pascal says, "It is good to be tired and weary from fruitlessly seeking the true good, so that one can stretch out one's arms to the Redeemer."[19]

Pascal can come to this conclusion because his view of reason is different from Unamuno's and is based on a different view of the human person. While Unamuno identifies "reason" in a positivistic way with what can be known by science, Pascal has a richer conception of reason. For Pascal reason can take on different qualities, depending on the character of the reasoner. There is a duality that Pascal sees in the human personality that cannot be escaped. We are wonderfully made in the image of God with God-like capacities, and we are also wretched folk whose capacity to do harm to others and ourselves is limitless. Our ability to reason is subject to the same duality. It can be used for good, and it can also be horribly flawed. Pascal recognizes both when he says, "One must know when it is right to doubt, to affirm, to submit. Anyone who does otherwise does not understand the force of reason. Some men run counter to these three principles, either affirming that everything can be proved, because they know nothing about proof, or doubting everything, because they do not know when to submit, or always submitting, because they do not know when judgment is called for."[20]

Unamuno sees the danger in affirming that everything can be proved as the dogmatist does and the danger in always submitting, as in the faith of *el carbonero*. But he does not seem to be able to judge when to submit, because he does not embrace Pascal's belief that reason can be flawed, that there are limits to his ability to know. Pascal says, "Reason's last step is the recognition that there are an infinite number of things which are beyond it. It is merely feeble if it does not go as far as to realize that. If natural things are beyond it, what are we to say about supernatural things?"[21] Unamuno says that he recognizes that the question of immortality lies outside the bounds of reason,

19. Ibid., 631:237.
20. Ibid., 170:83.
21. Ibid., 188:85.

as we will see shortly, but he does not happily accept any limits on his ability to know about the existence of God or the end of this life.

Is Kierkegaard gripped with doubt? We have already noted that Unamuno considered Kierkegaard a person who knew and lived the "tragic sense of life." In an essay entitled, "Ibsen y Kierkegaard," Unamuno states that Kierkegaard was a person full of "resignación desesperada" ("desperate resignation") (3:289). Kierkegaard shares with Unamuno a concern about authentic existence that is concrete, which matters both now and for eternity. In *Del sentimiento trágico de la vida* Unamuno quotes Kierkegaard's pseudonym, Climacus, to underscore his contention that the question of the immortality of the soul lies outside of reason, because reason, abstract thought, refuses to take the question seriously. The quote from *Concluding Unscientific Postscript* is worth reproducing, in part, here:

> The dubiousness of abstraction manifests itself precisely in the connection with all existential questions, from which abstraction removed the difficulty by omitting it and then boasts of having explained everything. It explains immortality in general, and see, it goes splendidly, inasmuch as immortality becomes identical with eternity, with the eternity that is essentially the medium of thought. But abstraction does not care about whether a particular existing human being is immortal, and just that is the difficulty. It is disinterested, but the difficulty of existence is the existing person's interest, and the existing person is infinitely interested in existing. Thus abstract thinking helps me with my immortality by killing me as a particular existing individual and then making me immortal and therefore helps somewhat as in Holberg the doctor took the patient's life with his medicine—but also drove out the fever (CUP 302).

Yes, Kierkegaard was concerned with immortality, and he also shared Unamuno's distrust in reason to dispel the uncertainty about the end of life. But Kierkegaard's angst is not caused simply by not knowing what would happen when he dies. Rather, Kierkegaard's anxiety is rooted in the human condition which includes the terrible freedom to have a relationship with God or to fail to do so. His book, *The Concept of Anxiety*, is about sin as it stems from anxiety and destroys a proper relationship between the infinite and the finite.

At this point it is important to counter a popular misconception about Kierkegaard's view of doubt and faith. It is not true that Kierkegaard would agree with Unamuno's claim that "Fe que no duda es fe muerta" (7:311).

("Faith that does not doubt is dead faith.") The doubt that Unamuno champions is equally applied to reason and faith. The life based on doubt will be a life of struggle, as quoted above, "El modo de vivir, de luchar, de luchar por la vida y vivir de la lucha, de la fe, es dudar" (7:311). ("The way to live, to struggle, to struggle for life and to live from the struggle, to life from faith, is to doubt.") While Kierkegaard eschews the kind of certainty that leads to dogmatism, he is far from promoting doubt as a way of life. Rather, Kierkegaard sees the need to act, even when there are known risks involved. In *Fragments* Climacus says, "When belief resolves to believe, it runs the risk that it was an error, but nevertheless it wills to believe. One never believes in any other way; if one wants to avoid risk, then one wants to know with certainty that one can swim before going into the water" (PF 83).

Though faith and doubt can exist in the same person for Kierkegaard—and thus are not mutually exclusive—they are "opposite passions." "Belief is the opposite of doubt. Belief and doubt are not two kinds of knowledge that can be defined in continuity with each other, for neither of them is a cognitive act, and they are opposite passions. Belief is a sense for coming into existence, and doubt is a protest against any conclusion that wants to go beyond immediate sensation and immediate knowledge. The doubter, for example, does not deny his own existence, but he draws no conclusions, for he does not want to be deceived" (PF: 84). Resolution is called for, even in the presence of risk. The Kierkegaardian leap is truly a leap and not just a matter of *querer creer* or wanting to believe. "The conclusion of belief is no conclusion [*Slutning*] but a resolution [*Beslutning*], and thus doubt is excluded" (PF: 84). Again, the opposite passion of doubt is faith. What is excluded is not uncertainty because that is part and parcel of faith. Rather, what is excluded, from Kierkegaard's point of view, is vacillation and mistrust. Although faith is a response to uncertainty, it is not an embrace of that uncertainty. To choose faith is to choose not to doubt. To illustrate the importance of this difference between Kierkegaard and Unamuno, let us look at each of their reactions to an issue already noted in the discussion of Pascal, that of the hiddenness of God.

In the chapter of *Del sentimiento trágico de la vida* entitled, "En el fondo del abismo" ("In the Depths of the Abyss"), Unamuno quotes his sonnet "La oración del ateo" ("The Prayer of the Atheist"). The poem serves as a poignant complaint to a God who is hidden, conceived as a prayer to a God who does not exist. Just the last *terceto* is quoted in the text, "Sufro a tu costa, / Dios no existente, pues si Tú existieras/ Existiría yo también de veras" (7:181). ("I suffer at your cost, / Non-existent God, for if you were to exist/I would also exist in reality.") Within the poem the greatness of God is diminished as the deity becomes nothing more than an Idea. The poetic voice decries this God who is the cause of his suffering, a God who, if he had made himself more evident, would guarantee the existence of the poet, as well.

Unamuno also reveals his frustration with a God who will not allow his face to be seen in his multiple references to the fact that Moses was denied the chance to see God's face. One of them is found in a play called, *La venda,* a story about a formerly blind woman, María, who refuses to take off the bandage that keeps her from seeing her father, whom she has only known through relationship and insight, not through sight. There is much to be mined from this play as it reveals the playwright's attitudes toward faith and reason, but our focus here is on the introduction to the action given by the characters Don Pedro and Don Juan.

Don Pedro and Don Juan represent the two warring factions in Unamuno's world view, reason and faith respectively. They are discussing living according to truth or according to illusion—living according to reason or according to faith. Don Pedro maintains that one must live according to the truth, while Don Juan counters that to do so is to die, and to live by illusion engenders life. Don Juan then refers to the Old Testament story about Moses desiring to see God and God refusing to let Moses see his face, because if he were to see the face of God, he would die.[22] When Don Juan intimates that the same thing might happen to us if we were allowed to see God, Don Pedro replies, "¡Qué hermosa muerte! ¡Morir de haber visto la verdad! ¿Puede apetecerse otra cosa?. . . la razón nos revela el secreto del mundo, la razón nos hace obrar" (5:224). ("What a beautiful death! To die as a result of having seen the truth! Can you want anything else? . . . reason reveals to us the secret of the world; reason makes us work.") One has the sense that Unamuno, though showing us the extremes of the views, agrees with Don Pedro. For him, truth should not be hidden, which Unamuno confirms in "¿Qué es verdad? (3:863). Man should know the secret of the world; it should not be denied him. By hiding himself, God denies us the truth.

There are, of course, other ways to read the text from Exodus. One can read God's refusal to let his face be seen as a mercy, as a kindness. Later in the Biblical text we find that God tells Moses that he will show him proofs of his kindness and he will allow him to know his name. And when God passes by he mercifully covers Moses' eyes, protecting him from death, but

22. Exodus 33:17–23.

he allows Moses to see his back. God allows Moses to see and to know what he is capable of knowing. Unamuno wants to know it all, and he believes that he should be able to know it all. He is offended by a God who would not let him see his face.

Why doesn't God dazzle us with his brilliance and make himself known, so that there would be no question about his existence? Many have asked the same question and Kierkegaard partially answers it in *Concluding Unscientific Postscript.* There he argues that God would not be revealing his true nature if he were to do such a thing as appear to us as "a rare, enormously large green bird with a red beak, that perched in a tree on the embankment and perhaps even whistled in an unprecedented manner" (CUP 245). The person who would be convinced by such a tawdry display might be impressed, but impressed with what? In *Philosophical Fragments* Kierkegaard answers the question more positively by emphasizing that what God wants in revealing himself to us is a relationship, a relationship that is based on freedom and trust. He illustrates his point by telling the story of the king who loved a humble maiden and wanted to woo her. Though he most certainly could have her as his wife by revealing his status, his riches and power, and all those around him would have told him that the girl would be fortunate for having been chosen, he does not want to coerce her or manipulate her into loving him. Rather, he comes to her disguised as a humble servant so that the relationship would be one of equality, not rank (PF 26–30). Likewise, for God to reveal himself to humankind requires a king who is hidden. The incarnation is the way God accomplishes this.

For Kierkegaard, God is hidden to some and partially hidden to others. The ability to see and know God has to do with certain characteristics of the person which he terms as "inwardness," or "subjectivity." "Nature, the totality of creation, is God's work, and yet God is not there, but within the individual human being there is a possibility (he is spirit according to his possibility) that in inwardness is awakened to a God-relationship, and then it is possible to see God everywhere" (CUP 246). Knowledge of God is linked with spiritual development.[23] That is not to say that knowledge of God is linked with education or intelligence. Spiritual development must be available to all persons, educated or not. It has more to do with moral development as one is aware of the good that one should do and one's inability to do the good without God's help. This is important because, "Linking the knowledge of God to the development of subjectivity ensures that coming

23. See C. S. Evans, "Can God Be Hidden?" 245.

to know God will be a process whereby I grow and flourish as a person."[24] The key here is humility and submitting to the authority of God. It is the ability to say that God may have good reason to remain hidden from me at any one moment, and the fact that I do not know that reason is due to my finitude and possibly my sinfulness, not to the fact that God is not there.

We have already noted that Pascal did experience the Psalmist's "dark night of the soul," knowing personally the despair of the hiddenness of God. At other points in the *Pensées* he speaks to the issue in ways that are consistent with his general view of the human condition and the proper relationship of the individual with God, given that condition. Once again, his general view of the human condition is that we by nature have two sides, one that is glorious because it is made in the image of God and one that is terribly flawed by the presence of sin. God reveals himself in ways that are consistent with our nature and his. "If there were no obscurity man would not feel his corruption: if there were no light man could not hope for a cure. Thus it is not only right but useful for us that God should be partly concealed and partly revealed, since it is equally dangerous for man to know God without knowing his own wretchedness as to know his wretchedness without knowing God."[25]

Pascal also notes that in the case of God incarnate, the coming of Jesus to earth, it was clearly predicted that his divinity would be hidden, even to some of those who saw him face to face. "What do the prophets say about Jesus Christ? That he will plainly be God? No, but that he is a truly hidden God, that he will be not recognized, that people will not believe that it is he, that he will be a stumbling-block on which many will fall."[26] So what determined who would see him as God and who would not? Pascal says what the New Testament does, that those who have ears to hear, hear. Jesus came to heal the sick, to call sinners to repentance while those who feel they are righteous and those who are rich will go away empty. Centuries after the fact, the divinity of Christ is perceived according to the heart of the person, just as it was when Jesus was first on earth. Pascal concludes, "Thus wishing to appear openly to those who seek him with all their heart and hidden from those who shun him with all their heart, he has qualified our knowledge of him by giving signs which can be seen by those who seek him

24. Ibid.
25. Pascal, *Pensées*, 446:167.
26. Ibid., 228:101.

and not by those who do not. There is enough light for those who desire only to see and enough darkness for those of a contrary disposition."[27]

The response of our three authors to the hiddenness of God allows us to bring into focus why it is that Unamuno was unable to make the leap of faith that Kierkegaard and Pascal made. The clear difference between Unamuno and the others is his view of reason and what it should be able to accomplish. Unamuno is offended by a God who would not allow him to see his face. In "La oración del ateo" ("The Prayer of the Atheist") we see an angry poet who is affronted by a God who does not make his existence known plainly. Both Kierkegaard and Pascal are wholly aware of the hiddenness of God, but see the individual as needing to learn something through it. They see human reason as limited and flawed and in need of revelation and grace. If we can for a moment equate the hiddenness of God with the paradox, we can say that Kierkegaard actually predicted Unamuno's response to the paradox when he pointed out in *Postscript* that the only true responses to the paradox are faith and offense. Unamuo is offended by the hiddenness of God because he sees no need for his ability to know to be challenged by revelation or changed by grace. He is therefore unable to make the leap of faith.[28] Unamuno is left, rather, with *querer creer* and with the agony of doubt and faith held in perpetual tension.

We began with Unamuno's claim that Kierkegaard and Pascal embody the tragic sense of life. It is true that Unamuno resonated with parts of their authorship and believed that they shared the essence of his agonic life. However, as I have shown, if one looks at how each author deals with the critical relationship between doubt and faith, significant differences come to light that mitigate against Unamuno's assertion that Kierkegaard and Pascal share his tragic sense of life. It is true that all three philosophers see real danger in claims of certainty that lead to dogmatism. None of the three sees much usefulness for logical proofs for God's existence. They all acknowledge the existence and importance of uncertainty in relationship to faith, but for Kierkegaard and Pascal uncertainty is not the same as doubt.

The doubt that Unamuno wants to apply equally to reason and to faith, which he sees as the life-force keeping the two in tension, becomes paralyzing for him with regard to faith. Unamuno recognizes the inability of

---

27. Ibid., 149:80.

28. Cerezo Galán, *Las máscaras*, 431, agrees saying, "Mas en Unamuno la paradoja no puede trascender el límite de la razón en el salto a la fe, y se queda en la tensión agónica misma." ("But in Unamuno the paradox cannot transcend the limits of reason in the leap of faith and he remains in the same, agonic tension.")

reason to decide matters like the existence of God or the knowledge of a life beyond this one. But, in truth, he chafes at that inability and believes that he should be able to know. This is demonstrated in his response of offense to the hiddenness of God as contrasted with the response of Kierkegaard and Pascal. Kierkegaard believes seeing God is a matter of inwardness and that God shows as much of himself to the person as the person is able to profitably grasp as he matures spiritually. Pascal cries out against a God who is hidden from him at times, but in the end, he sees his inability to see God as a result of his finitude and his own need of God's revelation and grace. With Martín Gelabert, I see no room for revelation in Unamuno's view.[29]

Querer creer (to want to believe) allows Unamuno to continue to doubt and not to commit. Unamuno is content with wanting to believe rather than making the leap of faith. Though he says that faith is a matter of the will, wanting to believe is enough for him, and therefore Unamuno is kept from embracing the faith of Kierkegaard and Pascal by retaining a doubt that privileges the struggle between reason and faith above faith itself.

29. See Gelabert, "Dios, exigencia y pregunta del hombre," 170, where he says that given Unamuno's presuppositions, "No hay sitio para la revelación en Unamuno." ("There is no place for revelation in Unamuno.")

6

The Unhealed Wound

Suffering in Unamuno and Kierkegaard

IT IS HARD FOR our contemporary culture to make sense of talk about the benefits of suffering. Daily we are offered a plethora of drugs, diets and practices to relieve physical and mental pain. Even within the Christian church, healing and an absence of pain have been marks of blessing and true faith from the late 19th century onward, particularly in Protestant circles.[1] Of course, it was not always so in Christianity. In earlier periods, bodily affliction was seen as a way to identify more closely with the suffering of Christ and as such, a road to Christian perfection. In addition to physical pain, enduring persecution, suffering for the sake of Christ, was seen as a special mark of a true Christian through most of the first two millennia and still is today in places where Christianity is not welcome.

Søren Kierkegaard wrote in the middle of the nineteenth century while Miguel de Unamuno wrote approximately fifty years later, as the nineteenth century turned into the twentieth. Both of these authors owe a debt to the early Christian tradition of the benefits of suffering as they bring those insights into their discussion on authentic existence and how it should be lived. To speak of authentic existence is to bring to mind the philosophy of existentialism. Unamuno has been linked to Kierkegaard through a line of thinkers identified as existentialists that began with Kierkegaard and runs through Sartre, even though the tenets of existentialism are imprecise and

---

1. For a detailed study of the change in the view of suffering in the United States, see Curtis, *Faith in the Great Physician: Suffering and Divine Healing in American Culture.*

it is questionable whether Kierkegaard has much in common with Sartre or other so called existentialists at all.

Unamuno was considered an existentialist philosopher as early as 1956,[2] and arguing the point is not within the scope of this study, but it is true that both Kierkegaard and Unamuno present the search for authentic being as a way to understand existence and live it. It is also true that both authors discuss the role of suffering in the development of authentic existence, and that they even use the same metaphor of the unhealed wound in order to explore the theme. We will see, however, that the two authors are not in agreement about the ends to which suffering works. The disagreement over the purposes of suffering reveals further disagreement over the fundamental goals of human life. For Unamuno, the ultimate objective of suffering is to increase consciousness so that the individual may better recognize the eternal and the beautiful. For Kierkegaard, suffering plays an important role in the renewal of the individual so that the person can become what God wants him or her to be.

To begin, let us examine the metaphor that both authors use to characterize the nature of suffering: the unhealed wound. The metaphor of the unhealed wound is found in *Concluding Unscientific Postscript*, one of the works of Kierkegaard that is most quoted by Unamuno. In Unamuno's copy of *Postscript*, next to the passage in which it appears, he has written the Danish word *saar* in the margin together with the words *herida* (injury) and *llaga* (wound) written in Spanish. In the quote in which the word *saar* appears, Johannes Climacus, Kierkegaard's pseudonym, says the following:

> But the genuine subjective existing thinker is always just as negative as he is positive and vice versa: he is always that as long as he exists, not once and for all in a chimerical mediation . . . He is cognizant of the negativity of the infinite in existence; he always keeps open the wound of negativity, which at all times is a saving factor (the others let the wound close and become positive—deceived); . . . He is, therefore, never a teacher, but a learner, and if he is continually just as negative as positive, he is continually striving (CUP 85).

The quote speaks about the way in which an individual, the genuine subjective thinker, deals with the two parts of his being, the temporal and the infinite. Climacus further explains by saying, "But what is existence? It is that child who is begotten by the infinite and the finite, the eternal and the temporal, and is therefore continually striving" (CUP 92). Kierkegaard

2. See Levi, "Quixotic Quest for Being," 135.

believes that these two elements of the individual must be synthesized in order to become an authentic self, but in this life the process never ends and is full of suffering. To fail to struggle is to fail to exist.

These are themes that resonate with the philosophy of Miguel de Unamuno. As we have seen, for him the struggle is between the head and the heart. The head—reason and science—tells us that life ends with death, but the heart demands that the person continue to live, and that he live as an individual, not as a part of some impersonal cosmos. The two poles struggle within the human being and from the struggle comes life itself. Unamuno says of himself in *Del sentimiento trágico de la vida* that he is a man of contradictions and that those contradictions unify his life and give him his reason for being (7:262). Those who do not think about the necessity of immortality don't deserve it. Those who don't participate in the struggle between the head and the heart are not living.

Much before the publication of *Del sentimiento trágico de la vida*, in his book of 1905, *Vida de don Quijote y Sancho,* Unamuno describes the purpose of his work in this way: "Hay que inquietar los espíritus y enfusar en ellos [los prójimos] fuertes anhelos, aun a sabiendas de que no han de alcanzar nunca lo anhelado" (3:155). ("One must disquiet the spirits [of one's neighbors] and infuse in them powerful longings, even in the knowledge that they will never achieve what they long for.") Reading further in the same work we discover Unamuno's use of the metaphor of the unhealed wound to define more precisely the objective of his work. The volume of Kierkegaard in which *Concluding Unscientific Postscript* appears was published in 1902, and it is reasonable to suppose that Unamuno had read the passage in which the unhealed wound appears before he wrote in *Vida de don Quijote y Sancho*: "Mira lector, aunque no te conozco, te quiero tanto que si pudiese tenerte en mis manos, te abriría el pecho y en el cogollo del corazón te rasgaría una llaga y te pondría allí vinagre y sal para que no pudieses descansar nunca y vivieras en perpetua zozobra y en anhelo inacabable" (3:241). ("Look, reader, though I do not know you, I love you so much that if I could hold you in my hands, I would open up your breast and in the center of your heart I would make a wound and into it I would put vinegar and salt, so that you might never rest again, and would live in continual anguish and endless longing.") Of course, it is not possible to prove the source for the metaphor of the unhealed wound, but we can certainly recognize the power of the metaphor to evoke the depth of the suffering that a person must experience in order to exist authentically. The two authors found in the wound a metaphor for suffering, and they are in agreement that there is something beneficial that comes from not allowing the wound to heal.

The unhealed wound defines suffering in a visceral, emotive way, but that is just a starting point. There is much more to be said about the meaning of suffering in Kierkegaard and Unamuno. In *Del sentimiento trágico de la vida* Unamuno says, "El dolor es la sustancia de la vida y la raíz de la personalidad, pues sólo sufriendo se es persona" (7:230). ("Pain is the substance of life and the root of personality. Therefore, only by suffering does one become a person.") For Unamuno, it is the desire for immortality that produces the suffering that defines existence. The heart demands that this life not end with death, and reason demands evidence of life after death, evidence that does not exist. For Unamuno, this pain is the angst that brings us to God, and it is a pain that is distinguished from physical pain. "El dolor nos dice que existimos; . . . y el dolor nos dice que existe y que sufre Dios; pero es el dolor de la congoja, de la congoja de sobrevivir y ser eternos. La congoja nos descubre a Dios y nos hace quererle" (7:232). ("Pain tells us that we exist . . . and pain tells us that God exists and suffers; but it is the pain of anguish, of the anguish of surviving and being eternal. Anguish reveals God for us and it makes us love him.") Enjoyment of life can hide reality, and therefore it should be avoided. "Cuando se goza olvídase uno de sí mismo, de que existe, pasa a otro, a lo ajeno, se en-ajena. Y sólo se ensimisma, se vuelve a sí mismo, a ser él en el dolor" (7:192). ("When a person enjoys himself, he forgets himself, that he exists, he becomes another person that is alien to himself. He only returns to his centered self through suffering.") The work of Unamuno consists in not allowing his readers to forget themselves.

Through suffering we come to know ourselves. Suffering makes us conscious of our limitations (7:192). Self-consciousness helps us to identify ourselves in relation to our neighbor so that we understand who we are and who we are not. But consciousness also helps us to realize that we will not last forever. To know that all is perishable and transitory helps us to value the eternal and the beautiful, and in this we can see the necessity of suffering. Unamuno says in the chapter entitled, "Fe, esperanza y caridad" ("Faith, Hope and Charity"), that suffering, in reality, gives hope. "Acongojados al sentir que todo pasa, que pasamos nosotros, que pasa lo nuestro, que pasa cuanto nos rodea, la congoja misma nos revela el consuelo de lo que no pasa, de lo eterno, de lo hermoso" (7:229). ("Anguished at feeling that everything passes away, that we pass away, that all that is ours passes away, that everything around us passes away, the anguish itself reveals to us the comfort of what does not pass away, the eternal and the beautiful.") Without the pain produced by the recognition of our finitude, we wouldn't know the eternal.

For Unamuno, suffering is important because God suffers. In the *Tratado de amor de Dios*, (*Treatise on Love of God*), Unamuno declares that the scandal of Christianity both for the Jews and for the Greeks, is that God became man and that he had to suffer to redeem men, "la eterna verdad ante la que se sienten los hombres aterrados, ésta es, . . . que enviaste a tu Hijo, al hijo de tus entrañas al hombre, a sufrir pasión y muerte y a redimirnos sufriendo."[3] ("the eternal truth before which all men feel terrified is this, that you sent your Son, the son of your heart, to men, to suffer passion and death and to redeem us, suffering.") The end result is that upon discovering the Son of God, men discovered through him that God is a God who suffers. In addition, "Quien no conoce al Hijo del hombre que sufre congojas de sangre, desgarramientos del corazón, dolor que mata y resucita, quien no conoce al Hijo no conocerá al Padre, ni sabrá de Dios, de Dios que sufre."[4] ("Whoever does not know the Son of man who suffers the anguish of blood and the tearing of his heart, pain that kills and brings to life again, whoever does not know the Son will not know the Father, nor will he know about God, the God who suffers.") Therefore, the person who would know the God who suffers must also suffer in order to obtain that knowledge. "Creer en Dios es amarle, y amarle es sentirle sufriente."[5] ("To believe in God is to love him, and to love him is to feel him as the suffering one.")

The importance of suffering extends to human relations. Through pain we can identify with our neighbor. Unamuno explains, "El dolor es lo trascendente, el dolor es la sustancia de la vida. Y el dolor es universal y es lo que a los seres todos nos une; es la sangre universal, divina, que por todos circula."[6] ("Pain is transcendent; pain is the substance of life. And pain is universal and it is what unites us human beings; it is the universal, divine blood that circulates through all.") We recognize in our neighbor the same misery that exists in our own soul. This misery is the beginning of self-compassion which in turn is the beginning of the ability to love oneself. Unamuno concludes,

---

3. Unamuno, *Tratado de amor*, 588.

4. Ibid.

5. Ibid., 591.

6. Ibid., 589.

"Y esta compasión, cuando es viva y sobreabundante, se vierte de mí en los demás, y del exceso de mi compasión propia compadezco a mis prójimos. La miseria propia es tanta que la compasión que despierta desborda pronto, y nos revela la miseria universal."[7] ("And this compassion, when it is alive and abundant, overflows from me to others, and from the excess of my own compassion, I have compassion for my neighbors.") To summarize Unamuno's view, suffering is necessary for me to know myself and for me to know God. In addition, suffering is necessary for me to understand my neighbor and my responsibility toward him or her.

For Kierkegaard there are three stages on the path that one should take in order to become an individual who lives authentically—the esthetic, the ethical and the religious. We are born into the esthetic stage. In that stage, we live to satisfy whatever desire we have, particularly when we are children. But there are many who continue in this stage as adults as they seek a series of unique "moments" to enjoy themselves and to avoid being bored. When people recognize that all of their "moments" are really hollow and meaningless, they realize that they do not have an integrated self. In order to have a true self, the self must choose his or her enduring passions. Enduring passions take the form of commitments, and this person who has committed himself to his enduring passions, then passes to the ethical stage.

Within the ethical stage, the person recognizes that there are obligations that one must meet. The source of those obligations is God, although it is possible that the person does not recognize the source.[8] At the point at which the person realizes that the ethical task is to become the person that God created him or her to be, a task which requires God's help, then the person is ready to pass into the religious stage. The religious stage has two steps, "religiousness A," which is a religion of immanence, and "religiousness B." In the stage of "religiousness B," the person confronts the God of history, Jesus, who must remake the person so that he or she can become the self created for him or her by God from creation.

The individual may suffer in all of the stages, but the suffering in the esthetic stage comes to the person from outside and is characterized as bad luck or misfortune that the person desires to avoid. However, in the ethical and the religious stages, suffering is a state which the individual does not seek to avoid. Unamuno marked for emphasis in the margin of *Postscript* a passage in which Climacus says, "Viewed religiously, the fortunate person,

---

7. Ibid., 592.

8. See C. S. Evans, "Divine Commands," especially 156–64.

whom the whole world favors, is just as much a suffering person, if he is religious, as the person to whom misfortune comes from outside" (CUP 436).

For Kierkegaard, the religious stage is particularly distinguished by suffering. It is here that we find the strong agreement with the thought of Unamuno. Explaining that to act religiously is to suffer, Climacus says, "Revelation is marked by mystery, eternal happiness [*Salighed*] by suffering, the certitude of faith by uncertainty, easiness by difficulty, truth by absurdity; if this is not maintained, then the esthetic and the religious merge in common confusion" (CUP 432n). Climacus associates positivity generally with the esthetic stage and characterizes it as being happy with the status quo and with a lazy enjoyment of life, much like we saw in Unamuno. Climacus says of the person who thinks subjectively, "He does not derive positive, cozy joy from life" (CUP 85).

The suffering of the religious stage is not self-inflicted. It is not associated with the ascetic practices or the monastic life. Kierkegaard respects the monastic life, but he fears that those who participate in it will believe that their actions of sacrifice will gain favor with God in this life and the next. What Kierkegaard wants to underscore is the necessity of divine transformation in life in order to become the person that God wants one to be. It is not by human works but by the work of God that that happens.

The suffering of the religious stage is characterized by the suffering that occurs when a person surrenders the relative for the absolute. If the relative, which could include a career or a good salary, is in conflict with the desire for the good, then the person suffers when he gives up the relative things. Suffering comes when a person realizes that he must die to himself in order to obtain eternal happiness, the absolute or the good—all names that Kierkegaard uses to explain the optimal relationship with God. This suffering occurs when the person recognizes and accepts that in reality he or she controls nothing, that his or her existence depends on God. A recognition of dependence shows that the person understands that he is the creature and that God is the creator, especially when the person by his own human nature wants to be God.[9]

Since this recognition doesn't happen just once but, rather, must be faced many times, we can see the nature of suffering as continual or constant. Climacus says, "Inwardness (the ethical and ethical-religious individual), however, comprehends suffering as essential" (CUP 434). It does

9. A more extensive explanation of suffering with regard to the religious stage will be found in chapter 7.

not surprise us that Unamuno underscores in his copy of *Postscript* the following quote: "The poet can explain (transfigure) all existence, but he cannot explain himself, because he does not want to become religious and comprehend the secret of suffering as the form of the highest life, higher than all good fortune and different from all misfortune" (CUP 444). The poet here refers to the person in the esthetic stage. It seems that Unamuno affirms the sentiment expressed by Climacus.

Although these passages from *Postscript, Del sentimiento trágico de la vida* and *Vida de don Quijote y Sancho* reveal a tremendous amount of agreement between Kierkegaard and Unamuno, it is important to draw attention to some discrepancies in their views of the nature of suffering. The two images of the wound help us to see a fundamental difference. It is a normal expectation that a wound be cured in a healthy body. Ordinarily, it is a desired and hoped for result. Kierkegaard and Unamuno claim that there is something valuable in allowing the wound to be left unhealed, but Unamuno not only does not want the wound to heal, he wants to increase the pain by adding salt and vinegar into the wound. For Unamuno, the pain that is produced is the pain of war for which there is no peace.

There is a fundamental difference between the two authors in their view of whether to seek a cure. Kierkegaard believes that one should seek to be healed, but never be deceived that one has been entirely healed, and therefore the wound should remain open. Unamuno does not want himself, or anyone else to be healed. For Unamuno, there is no possibility of synthesizing the infinite and the temporal in this life, and the Spanish philosopher rejects the attempt to do so vehemently. Here there is a clear parting of the ways between Unamuno and Kierkegaard, who thought that authentic existence could only happen when the temporal and the infinite in our lives come into synthesis. At the beginning of *Sickness Unto Death*, Kierkegaard's pseudonym, Anti-Climacus, says, "A human being is a synthesis of the infinite and the finite, or the temporal and the eternal, of freedom and necessity, in short, a synthesis" (SUD 127). The process of arriving at this synthesis is full of pain, and full synthesis may not be reachable short of eternity, but the goal is clear, and it is important for the individual to be working toward the goal.

For Unamuno, synthesis is not possible, neither is it desirable. Rather, as we saw in chapter 5, Unamuno wants for his faith and reason to fight constantly on (7:180). He scorns the intellectuals who cannot feel this tension, as well as the *carbonero*, the coal delivery man, who never questions his existence. Neither of those wants to accept the suffering of the tragic sense of life.

As we first saw in chapter 2, in *La agonía del cristianismo*, Unamuno speaks of the struggle in Biblical terms. There Unamuno quotes the passage from St. Luke in which Jesus says that he did not come to bring peace but a sword. Unamuno admits that there are other passages which reflect the peace that the Gospel is supposed to produce, but his focus is on the peace that brings war and its relationship with doubt and faith. As we explored in chapter 5, Unamuno's emphasis is on the Spanish vision of Christ who not dead; he is agonizing. It is the Christ who says, "My God, my God, why have you forsaken me?" This is the vision that Unamuno maintains as he says that life is struggle and the essence of faith is to doubt. Struggle will always produce suffering and the more one suffers the more profoundly one understands existence. Recalling the conclusions of the previous chapter on the role of doubt in faith, Kierkegaard's view is not Unamuno's. Kierkegaard says that doubt and faith are opposite passions that exclude each other. "Faith is the opposite of doubt. Faith and doubt are not two kinds of knowledge that can be defined in continuity with each other, for neither of them is a cognitive act, and they are opposite passions" (PF 84).

Where does the continual focus on war come from in Unamuno? Nelson Orringer underscores the strong influence of Hegel in the thought of Unamuno. He explains the need for struggle in Unamuno in Hegelian terms, "Unamuno's thinking being, springing from a will to live (which we may call a Hegelian thesis), clashes with the annihilating force of reasoned religious doubt (conceived as an antithesis), and the contradiction gets internalized as the crux of his existence—his *Werden,* his becoming, his maturing (synthesis), his ever-renewed attempt to harmonize faith and reason on higher levels of reflection."[10] For Unamuno the goal is struggle, and the struggle continues in order to produce, "ever higher levels of reflection."

Here we have another significant parting of the ways for Unamuno and Kierkegaard. For Kierkegaard, the struggle is termed "striving" and is considered to be absolutely necessary, as in Unamuno. The person living authentic existence is one who, "is striving infinitely, is continually in the process of becoming, something that is safeguarded by his being just as negative as positive" (CUP 91). However, it is important to note in Kierkegaard that "the process of becoming" is working toward a goal. The goal is the synthesis of the infinite and the finite. The striving is the means to that

10. Orringer, "Translator's Introduction" to Unamuno, *Treatise on Love of God,* xv.

end, not an end in itself. In continually striving the individual retains a true sense of self and a proper perspective between the creature and the creator. It is a perspective in which the person surrenders to a God who needs to transform the person from the outside, not through the person's own efforts to obtain eternity.

There is also a different point of view in Kierkegaard about the suffering of Christ. Remember that Unamuno has quoted scripture in saying that in order to know God the father, one must know his Son, Christ, and share in his suffering. Even though Kierkegaard would say that we will know God better through suffering, he maintains that our suffering can never be analogous to the suffering of Christ. Climacus says, "Just as the suffering of the ordinary martyrs is not any analogy to Christ's, so also the believer's suffering is not, and the absolute paradox is indeed distinguishable in that every analogy is a deception" (CUP 598). For Kierkegaard, the incarnation is the absolute paradox because it includes the claim that God, who is eternal, has become human, who is temporal. The paradox rests on the tension between existence and eternity, and therefore we cannot compare our suffering to Christ's.

For Kierkegaard, God is not merely a God who suffers, but rather is a God of love who became man in order to suffer so that we could be restored to wholeness. Love was the motivation; suffering was the means to an end. The relationship between love and suffering in Unamuno is different. Unamuno's definition of love reflects his valuing the struggle above all. "No hay verdadero amor sino en el dolor, y en este mundo hay que escoger o el amor, que es el dolor, o la dicha . . . Desde el momento en que el amor se hace dichoso, se satisface, y ya no es amor . . . El hombre es tanto más hombre, esto es, tanto más divino, cuanta más capacidad para el sufrimiento, o mejor dicho, para la congoja, tiene . . . Es el amor, en fin, la desesperación resignada" (7:231). ("There is no true love save in suffering, and in this world one must choose either love, which is suffering, or happiness . . . From the moment in which love becomes happy, becomes satisfied, it is no longer love . . . Man is the more man—that is, the more divine—the greater his capacity for suffering or, rather, for anguish . . . Love is, in the end, resigned despair.") Unamuno calls God, "total Consciousness," and suffering is what brings about consciousness. "Dios no es sino el Amor que surge del dolor universal y se hace conciencia" (7:225). ("God is simply the Love that springs from universal suffering and becomes consciousness.")

Clearly, for Kierkegaard, the suffering of a human being serves different ends. Armand Baker can help us to further understand the discrepancy in the goal of suffering in Unamuno and Kierkegaard. In his insightful article, "The God of Miguel de Unamuno," Baker says, "Unamuno concludes that there will always be a state of tension between what is, and what is possible, and that a certain amount of conflict or, as he puts it, pain and suffering, will always exist to promote further expansion and creativity."[11] Baker identifies the state in which this further expansion and creativity happens as Unamuno's "eternal purgatory," about which he speaks in *Del sentimiento trágico de la vida*. However, Baker maintains that the desire for "eternal purgatory" has been Unamuno's hope for the future from the beginning of his life as an author. Baker quotes from Unamuno. "Y el alma, mi alma al menos, anhela . . .[un] eterno acercarse sin llegar nunca, inacabable anhelo, eterna esperanza que eternamente se renueva sin acabarse del todo nunca. Y con ello un eterno carecer de algo y un dolor eterno. Un dolor, una pena, gracias a la cual se crece sin cesar en conciencia y en anhelo . . . Un eterno Purgatorio, pues, más que una Gloria; una ascensión eterna" (7:260). ("And the soul, my soul at least, longs for . . . eternally coming near without ever arriving, inexhaustible longing, eternal hope that eternally is renewed without ever ceasing. And with it, an eternal lack of something, an eternal suffering. A suffering, a pain, thanks to which one grows in consciousness and longing without ceasing . . . An eternal purgatory, well, more than a glory, an eternal ascension.")

For Unamuno, this "eternal lack of something" that is "an eternal suffering," produces a growth "without end in consciousness." The purpose of the growth in consciousness in Unamuno is to obtain, "ever higher levels of reflection" according to Orringer. Baker expresses the purpose as "to promote further expansion and creativity." To confirm the opinion of these critics we need only to return to the statement quoted above from Unamuno that says, "Acongojados al sentir que todo pasa, que pasamos nosotros, que pasa lo nuestro, que pasa cuanto nos rodea, la congoja misma nos revela el consuelo de lo que no pasa, de lo eterno, de lo hermoso" (7:229). ("Anguished at feeling that everything passes away, that we pass away, that all that is ours passes away, that everything around us passes away, the anguish itself reveals to us the comfort of what does not pass away, the eternal and the beautiful.") In higher levels of reflection one can recognize and value the beautiful creatively. If the goal of suffering is to

11. Baker, "God of Miguel de Unamuno," 831.

widen our consciousness so that we recognize the eternal and the beautiful better, then it makes some sense that the metaphorical wound of which Unamuno speaks not only remain unhealed, but that there be an increase of the pain by pouring salt and vinegar into it.

On the other hand, Kierkegaard always maintains that suffering comes from the failure to become a self, and it is necessary as the first step to becoming an authentic self. For Kierkegaard, the purpose of suffering has to do with the transformation of the individual. It is true that both Unamuno and Kierkegaard do not see an end to suffering in this life. But for Kierkegaard, the continual nature of suffering has to do with the need that the person has to seek to be cured daily; he or she never stops seeking the cure. The recognition of the need is essential because the person who recognizes it will seek the help of God. The person who recognizes his or her need accepts his or her dependency on something or someone outside of himself or herself.

In *The Sickness Unto Death*, Anti Climacus speaks of the despair that results from not becoming a self. He is not talking about common despair which everyone experiences over the circumstances of life that are unpleasant. Rather, he speaks of two types of despair that keep a person from becoming a self. The first type of despair is not to want to be the self that God wants the person to be. This type of despair is essentially passive. It is a failure to even care about being a self or the failure to rouse oneself to begin such a task. The second type of despair is to want to be the self that the person chooses, rebelling against what God wants him or her to be. The second type of despair is active, and the person who experiences this type of despair wants more than anything to be the creator of himself or herself. Kierkegaard explains such an individual in this way: "He does not want to put on his own self, does not want to see his given self as his task— he himself wants to compose his self by means of being the infinite form" (SUD 68). A person in this state refuses to humble himself to be helped and believes that his suffering is unique.

Now, in *Sickness Unto Death,* despair is clearly called sin, and as such, would not be the wound that should remain open. But Kierkegaard also sees despair as a recognition of one's true state without God, and without despairing of one's own abilities to be come a self, one would never be the self God created the person to be. The opposite of despair is faith, but there is a kind of despair, a despair over one's own ability to achieve the goal of existence through autonomous striving, that is a necessary precondition for faith. This despair opens us up to faith because it helps us see our complete dependence on God. By faith an individual can be healed, can become the person that God has created him or her to be. The cure is God's work, not ours. It is our responsibility to keep the wound open so that we can receive God's healing at every moment.

We end where we began with the metaphor of the wound. Both Kierkegaard and Unamuno use the wound to express something essential in human life. The wound represents a source for experiencing authentic existence through suffering. The two authors are in agreement that suffering does not end in this life, that the wound is never cured, but the two authors see suffering serving different ends. Kierkegaard only wants for the wound to remain open so that the individual not cease to seek to be healed. The goal of suffering is the synthesis of an integrated self, the synthesis of the eternal and the temporal found in a relationship with the absolute, with God. Unamuno does not want for the wound to be healed and goes further to want to increase the pain of the wound with salt and vinegar. The goal for suffering can't be the synthesis of the eternal and the temporal because for him, those two entities must maintain war against each other during all of life. For Unamuno, suffering widens consciousness and with that, the ability to recognize and appreciate the eternal and the beautiful grows.

In an article entitled, "Ibsen y Kierkegaard," Unamuno says that Kierkegaard was a person full of "desesperación resignada," "resigned despair," all his life (3:289). It is possible that Kierkegaard was such a person, but it is necessary to recognize that the two authors understood the nature and the end of suffering very differently. And in those differences lie the profoundly distinct attitudes of Kierkegaard and Unamuno about life and about God.

7

Unamuno's Faith
and Kierkegaard's Religiousness A

Making Sense of the Struggle

THROUGHOUT THIS STUDY OF Unamuno's quest for faith I have brought to
light some of the affinities between Kierkegaard's and Unamuno's thought,
and I have sought to outline the significant differences. In chapter 2 we
saw that although Kierkegaard and Unamuno agree on the fact that truth
must be lived, they disagree on the possibility of objective truth. In chapter 5 we saw that while Pascal, Kierkegaard and Unamuno respect the
fact that uncertainty will always be a part of faith, Pascal and Kierkegaard make a leap of faith that Unamuno's sense of reason prohibits him
from making, preferring to claim that *querer creer*, wanting to believe,
is enough. In the previous chapter we saw that though Kierkegaard and
Unamuno recognize the need for the individual to suffer to achieve authentic existence, the fact that Unamuno wants for the wound to remain
open and to never be healed sets him apart from Kierkegaard who asks
only that the individual be constantly open to the God who can heal,
the God who can synthesize the temporal and the eternal. With these
significant differences highlighted here, one might think that Kierkegaard
would be very critical of Unamuno's stance. In this chapter I will show
that although there are deep differences in the thought of the two philosophers, there is deep appreciation in the Kierkegaadian corpus for the
character of Unamuno's faith.

Unamuno wrote his essay on faith, "La fe," soon after his spiritual crisis in 1897. That essay begins with a quote from Ibsen, "*Liv og tro skal smelte sammen,*" "Life and faith must meld together into one" (1:962). The quote from Ibsen leads us to Kierkegaard and back to the the the sequence of events that led to Unamuno's reading Kierkegaard. In a letter to Clarín, Unamuno reveals that he is immersing himself in reading the Danish theologian Kierkegaard whom he learned about through Brandes, who claimed that Ibsen aspired to be Kierkegaard's poetical voice.[1] To begin his essay on faith Unamuno uses Ibsen, who gives voice to Kierkegaard. The clear Kierkegaardian theme that runs through Unamuno's early essay on faith is that assent to a set of propositions cannot be called faith. Rather, to have faith is to live in hope and to work for an ideal, an ideal that is always in the future and will be for eternity. There is much more that can be gleaned from Kierkegaard's spheres of existence, and particularly Religiousness A, that can illuminate Unamuno's life of faith which is essentially a life of struggle.[2]

As we have noted, the Kierkegaardian text that has the most underlined passages and the text that is most quoted by Unamuno is *Concluding Unscientific Postscript.*[3] The existence spheres of the aesthetic and the ethical are artfully set forth in *Either/Or*, but it is in *Postscript* that the first two stages are compared with religiousness, the last of Kierkegaard's three stages of existence. It is in Kierkegaard's understanding of the stage of religiousness that we can situate the faith of Unamuno and through that understanding appreciate its intricacy and intensity. It is important to remember the trajectory of all of the stages before explicating the stage of religiousness more fully, even though the existence spheres were introduced in the previous chapter.

For Kierkegaard these three stages, the esthetic, the ethical and the religious, mark the progress of a person who is striving to live authentically. All of us begin in the esthetic stage where one lives for one's appetites and desires to be immediately satisfied. It is a stage in which one seeks to avoid boredom at all cost, and so the novel and the original are held in highest

---

1. Alas, *Epistolario a Clarín*, 82.

2. In "Unamuno, Nietzsche and Religious Modernism," Michael Gómez attributes Unamuno's need for holding contradictory views in tension to the modernism that grips both Unamuno and Nietzsche. I don't argue that point, but his explanation of the source of the philosophical struggle does not help to make sense of the struggle existentially, which is the focus of this chapter.

3. See chapter 3 n. 2 for an explanation of the relationship between Kierkegaard and his pseudonym, Climacus.

regard. The epitome of the esthete is the seducer whose diary is recorded at the end of *Either/Or*. The next stage begins when the esthete realizes that his or her life is just a succession of vacuous moments that do not really amount to happiness; then the person is poised to move on to the ethical stage. In *Either/Or* II Judge William seeks to convince "A," the writer of *Either/Or* I, that it is only when one begins to make commitments, exemplified by the commitment of marriage, that life acquires meaning. It is in this stage, the ethical stage, that one takes stock of one's passions and fulfills duties based on those passions. However, for Judge William, ethical passions are defined within the limits of societal expectations. The third stage is that of the religious, in which one realizes that the ethical life is unattainable in one's own strength. The religious life is divided into two more types, Religiousness A and Religiousness B. Religiousness A is a natural religion of immanence; Religious B is the transcendent religion of Christianity.

My purpose here is to illuminate Unamuno's faith with the content of Religiousness A. The fact that I am using Religiousness A and not Religiousness B is telling. Jesús-Antonio Collado in his book, *Kierkegaard y Unamuno: La existencia religiosa,* has done a careful and detailed study to show how Kierkegaard's view of faith is not shared by Unamuno. The view of faith that Collado attributes to Kierkegaard is orthodox Christianity, the basic beliefs found in the Nicene Creed. By arguing that Unamuno's faith is not Kierkegaard's Collado has convincingly demonstrated that Unamuno's faith is not Christian when contrasted with those basic beliefs. However, Collado seems dismissive of any substantive content in Unamuno's faith when he says that it is "una concepción incoherente y falta de madurez en que el nervio de las ideas resulta en el fondo desde el principio hasta el fin pobre y deleznable."[4] ("an incoherent concept and lacks maturity in that the core of the ideas is in essence poor and brittle from beginning to end.") I believe that Unamuno's faith does have significant meaning and that the Kierkegaardian category of Religiousness A, which Collado does not consider, can help to reveal its depth. But before we delve into Religiousness A, it is necessary to return to the existence stages and to further explicate what Kierkegaard means by the ethical stage. If we were to only use *Either/Or* as the basis of what Kierkegaard believes the ethical to be, we would be very mistaken.

In *Either/Or* and also in *Fear and Trembling* the practical, ethical life is seen as what one is expected to do as a reasonable, decent human being

---

4. Collado, *Kierkegaard y Unamuno*, 410.

within the context of a particular societal group.[5] However, in *Postscript* the ethical has a much richer content, one that goes beyond the ethics of Judge William. Here the ethical is still considered the second stage on the path to authentic existence, but we see that authentic existence may be in conflict with the societal expectations of citizenly duties. Johannes Climacus, the pseudonymous author of *Postscript*, says, "Ethics focuses upon the individual, and ethically understood it is every individual's task to become a complete human being, just as it is the presupposition of ethics that everyone is born in the condition of being able to become that" (CUP 346). For Climacus, the origin of the ethical mandate is God; it is God who calls the individual to be the person that he or she was created to be. However, it is entirely possible to feel the weight of the ethical task without knowing that it is God who has given the call. C. Stephen Evans says, "If God is the source of the ethical "ought," then anyone who is aware of the moral task already has an implicit awareness of God's reality, even if the individual does not recognize that is it God who is addressing him."[6]

In *Upbuilding Discourses in Various Spirits* Kierkegaard explains the ethical in terms of its goal—to be the person that one is supposed to be.[7] In order for the person to be what one should be, one must be single minded, one must will to do the "Good". The "Good" is what God wants of me. "At every person's birth there comes into existence an eternal purpose for that person, for that person in particular. Faithfulness to oneself in relation to this is the highest thing a person can do" (UDVS 129). Climacus sets forth this principle first in *Postscript* and clearly sees the beginning of the religious life in the ethical because the source of the ethical task is God. He says, "It is really the God-relationship that makes a human being a human being" (CUP 244). Since this is so, it is important to situate Unamuno first in the ethical sphere.

In his Danish copy of another of the *Upbuilding Discourses*, Unamuno writes as a summary in the margin, "Y es el fin de la vida hacerse un alma," "the end of life is to become a soul." The context is a discourse on the virtue of patience in the process of gaining one's soul. The theme resonated with Unamuno. In *Del sentimiento trágico de la vida* he writes, "Me dicen que he

5. These distinctions are made by C. S. Evans in *Kierkegaard: An Introduction*. I am indebted to his explication of the ethical and the religious found in chapter 6, "Religious existence: Religiousness A," 110–38.

6. Ibid., 115.

7. A section of this book is translated into English separately as *Purity of Heart is to Will One Thing.*

venido a realizar no sé qué final social; pero yo siento que yo, lo mismo que cada uno de mis hermanos, he venido a realizarme, a vivir" (7:116). ("They tell me that I have come to realize I don't know what social end; but I feel that I, the same as each one of my brothers, have come to realize myself, to live.") There is a clear sense that the obligation is to become what one is supposed to be as an individual, and not merely to serve some socially recognizable end. Unamuno's view here seems very close to that of Kierkegaard, who stresses the idea that a genuine ethical individual has a quality that he calls "primitivity," something that a person who lives only by conforming to social roles does not have (SUD 33). As early as *Concluding Unscientific Postscript* Kierkegaard had satirized the person who lacks individuality as similar to a child who does not know the rules of etiquette, and must first observe what others do at a dinner party before eating anything (CUP 244).

A person in the ethical stage is ready to pass on to the religious stage when one recognizes that one falls short of fulfilling one's commitments and when one recognizes the difficulty of the process of becoming a self, of gaining a soul. Religiousness A, in turn, has three "moments" that are also incremental steps in the deepening of the religious stage. They are resignation, suffering and guilt. Climacus calls them respectively, the "initial," "the essential," and the "decisive" moments of the religious stage designated as Religiousness A (CUP ix). Each of these will be explored individually, and I will outline their reflection in Unamuno's writings. We will see that Unamuno's thought most certainly embodies the first two of these steps while the last remains open to question.

The initial step is resignation which has to do with the person's relationship to "the absolute." If authentic existence is to be won by becoming the person one is intended to be, it is to be accomplished by willing the "highest good." Only then, according to Climacus, will a person have "an absolute relation to the absolute" and a "relative relation to the relative" (CUP 387.) For Climacus the absolute is equated with "eternal happiness," and it is contrasted with such relative goods as "a good job, a beautiful wife, health" (CUP 391). Those relative things are to be resigned if they come into conflict with "eternal happiness." What this means is that the person recognizes what is absolute, and sees what is most important in relationship to which all other things become dispensable. Climacus says, "If it does not absolutely transform his existence for him, then he is not relating himself to an eternal happiness; if there is something he is not willing to give up for its sake, then he is not relating himself to an eternal happiness" (CUP 393).

While Climacus designates the absolute as an "eternal happiness," Unamuno equates the absolute with immortality, essentially the same thing with the same demand on the person's existence. All other desires for Unamuno are subordinate to the desire for immortality. He says in the chapter entitled "El hambre de la inmortalidad" ("The Hunger for Immortality"), of *Del sentimiento trágico de la vida*, "El hambre de Dios, la sed de eternidad, de sobrevivir, nos ahogará siempre este pobre goce de la vida que pasa y no queda" (7:135). "The hunger for God, the thirst for eternity, for surviving, will drown us always in this poor enjoyment of life that passes and does not remain.") As we have seen throughout this study, the problem of immortality is the central problem around which Unamuno's entire work is woven. He puts it simply when he says, "Si muero, ya nada tiene sentido" (7:129). ("If I die, nothing makes sense now.") For Unamuno there is no meaning in this life if there is not another life in which the self he currently is remains.

There is no doubt but that Unamuno was willing to give up everything to face the problem of immortality squarely and to get others to face it as well. As we saw in chapter 4, he dismisses facile answers to the problem of immortality. As a scholar formed in the nineteenth century Unamuno rejects the notion that all intellectual endeavors contribute in some way to "progress" and thus we never die (8:835). Unamuno also discards pantheism in his discussion of individual conscience in *Del sentimiento trágico de la vida*. He says that being part of some unnamable mass of being before we were born and returning to it when we die annihilates any sense of individuality and therefore any sense of meaningful immortality (7:161). As we saw in chapter 4, in the *Diario íntimo* Unamuno calls living on in our children or in our publications "sad comfort." We might hope that our memory stays alive in the minds of kin and readers, but it is unreasonable to think our memory endures because each generation forgets much of what and who have gone before, just as we have forgotten our forebears (8:48). Progress, pantheism, living on in our children or our work, are all inadequate to satisfy the desire we have to live after death.

The image that Unamuno invokes in *Del sentimiento trágico de la vida* is that of staring down the Sphinx. "El remedio es considerarlo cara a cara, fija la mirada en la mirada de la Esfinge, que es así como se deshace el maleficio de su aojamiento. Si del todo morimos todos, ¿para qué todo? . . . Es el ¿para qué de la Esfinge" (7:134). ("The remedy is to consider it face to face, fix your gaze on the gaze of the Sphinx, that is the way to destroy the spell of its evil eye. If we all die from all of it, what purpose does it serve?

. . . It is the question of the Sphinx.") We have seen in *Vida de don Quijote y Sancho* that Unamuno speaks about his mission to awake his readers to the longing for immortality (3:155). With Don Quijote, Unamuno is not afraid of appearing absurd or ridiculous. He says, "Sólo el que ensaya lo absurdo es capaz de conquistar lo imposible . . . Y sobre todo, no hay más que un modo de triunfar de veras: arrostrar el ridículo" (3:141). ("Only he who undertakes the absurd is capable of conquering the impossible . . . And over all, there is no more than one way to really triumph: to brave the ridiculous.") The Church rejected his writings and encouraged the faithful not to read him, but Unamuno maintained his focus on immortality as the absolute through which all of our being must be defined. For Unamuno all other considerations are relative to that absolute, fulfilling the requirement of the first movement of Religiousness A.

The second aspect of Religiousness A that is outlined by Climacus in *Concluding Unscientific Postscript* is that of suffering. When a person gives up the relative for the absolute the result is suffering, as we saw in chapter 6. Climacus calls this kind of suffering "dying to immediacy," and it is different from the suffering that one would experience as a result of illness or catastrophe in one's life (CUP 499). Climacus says, "Fortune, misfortune, fate, immediate enthusiasm, despair—these are what the esthetic life-view has at its disposal" (CUP 434); these are not religious suffering but what he calls esthetic suffering. One can think of a perfect example of esthetic suffering from one of Unamuno's protagonists—Joaquín of *Abel Sánchez*. Joaquín is consumed by envy and hate that are the source of his constant suffering, but his is not religious suffering; it is esthetic suffering surrounding the circumstances of personal proclivities and the pain of unrequited love.

For Climacus, even the hurt that is felt in, say, the loss of a spouse, might or might not be religious suffering. If the loss points the individual ever more to the absolute, then this common suffering can become religious suffering. Fundamentally, religious suffering is about recognizing one's limits and one's dependence on God. Joaquín's suffering does the opposite. Rather than recognizing the need for God's help in his pain, Joaquín revels in his pain and sees himself as some sort of tragic hero. The religious suffering of which Climacus writes also cannot be equated with masochism or self-inflicted pain, as in self-flagellation, as though the point were just to make life miserable. The reason this is so is that people who torment themselves still see themselves as capable of accomplishing something important on their own; they have not learned that they must depend on God (CUP 463).

The pain of religious suffering is ongoing because the relinquishing of the relative to the absolute is never finished. So Climacus characterizes all of the religious life as one of suffering. "Just as the faith of immediacy is in fortune, so the faith of the religious is in this, that life lies precisely in suffering" (CUP 436). We have seen that the heart of Unamuno's life of struggle is suffering because the desire for immortality can never be fulfilled. All that is vital points to life after death but all that is rational denies that possibility. Faith wants to believe what reason rejects, and life must be lived in the tension between the two. The result is suffering and pain which makes us aware of our own existence and the desire to go on living. For Unamuno the pain of suffering is necessary and can bring us to hope in the eternal. Without facing our finitude and the suffering that results from that, we would not know the eternal.

According to Climacus, a key to the life of suffering in Religiousness A is the recognition of our dependence on God to fulfill the demands of the ethical. Does Unamuno's faith include such dependence? Though Unamuno is accused of being arrogant, proud and defiant, he unequivocally points to our need for God when he says, "Y necesitamos a Dios para salvar la conciencia; no para pensar la existencia, sino para vivirla; no para saber por qué y cómo es, sino para sentir para qué es. El amor es un contrasentido si no hay Dios" (7:201). ("And we need God to save consciousness; not to think about existence but to live it; not to know the why and the how of it but to believe for what purpose it serves. Love is nonsense if there is no God.") Unamuno realizes that in order to have immortality there needs to be a God but rationally proving God is beyond human reason (7:204). Since our thirst to know God rationally will never be assuaged and the desire for immortality should always motivate our minds and our hearts, the suffering and struggle should never end and will never end. As we saw in chapter 6, the wound should be kept open and never be healed (3:241). Unamuno's view certainly seems to conform to Climacus' view that the religious life is one of continual suffering.

The last step in the existence sphere of Religiousness A, according to Climacus, is that of the personal recognition of guilt. He takes some care to explain what he means by guilt. The guilt of which he speaks is acknowledgement of one's failure to become what God has intended and the recognition that only God can provide the means to assuage that guilt.

He outlines different views of guilt which do not reach the level of religious guilt. First, guilt could be viewed as personal failures that do not require God for their solution. Second, guilt could be viewed as crimes for which civil punishment is appropriate. Finally, guilt could be understood as lapses in moral behavior for which one might do penance. In all these cases, the person would not require God for absolution. In religious guilt the person must recognize that there is ultimately nothing that one can do humanly to make up for or "solve" the ongoing failing to live up to what God wants him or her to be. The individual must recognize his utter dependence on God to remake the broken relationship between them.

It is at this step that there is some difficulty in wholly squaring Unamuno's faith with Kierkegaard's Religiousness A. There is evidence of Unamuno's having read the part of *Concluding Unscientific Postscript* in which Climacus outlines the requirements of this decisive step in Religiousness A. In a section in which Climacus deals with the fact that guilt "belongs essentially in the religious sphere," Unamuno underlined, "The religious address deals essentially with the totality-category. It can use a crime, it can use a weakness, it can use a negligence, in short, any particular whatever; but what sets the religious address apart as such is that it moves from this particular to the totality-category by joining this particular together with a relation to an eternal happiness" (CUP 538). The paragraph which starts with that quote ends with another underlined section that reads, "the religious address deals with inwardness, in which the totality-category seizes a person" (583). It would seem that Unamuno's attention was caught by the idea of the religious being faith that is wholly lived, that is related to "an eternal happiness." These are points of agreement between Unamuno and Kierkegaard.

But the idea of personal guilt and the need for God to restore a broken relationship between the human individual and himself seems not to be part of Unamuno's makeup. One thinks of a telling scene from *San Manuel Bueno, mártir* that is indicative of Unamuno's attitude toward personal culpability. Angela comes to Don Manuel with a question that has come to her as she was praying to Mary, "Mother of God, pray for us sinners now and in the hour of our death" after a holy week communion during which Don Manuel had asked her to pray for him. Upon praying the prayer she asked herself, "Us sinners? What is our sin, what?" and not being able to answer, she goes to Don Manuel. His response echoes Calderón de la Barca's *La vida es sueño* (*Life is a dream,*) as he says, "el delito mayor del hombre es haber nacido." ("The greatest sin of man is having been born.") Just in case she missed his meaning Don Manuel repeats, "Ese es, hija, nuestro pecado: el haber nacido" (2:1147). ("That is our sin, child: having been born.") Our problem is our finitude, our very existence.

Interestingly, Kierkegaard anticipated such a response to guilt. In *Postscript* Climacus explains that since guilt is a universal phenomenon that is grounded in the gap between the eternal and our temporal actuality, it is tempting to "shove the guilt onto the one who placed him in existence or onto existence itself" (CUP 528). In this case, guilt is made to be an ontological problem rather than a moral or a personal failure. Kierkegaard says that the most decisive expression of Religiousness A is a person who refuses to use this excuse and who thus sees himself or herself as truly guilty. Unamuno, however, seems to see the gap between ideal and achievement as inherent in existence rather than something for which one should take responsibility. Our sin is that of having been born. Climacus says that on this view, "the guilt-consciousness is only a new expression for suffering in existence," and so the person holding this view has only come to the second step of Religiousness A and not to the third (CUP 528).

My intent here has been to show the richness and the depth of Unamuno's faith through the lens of Kierkegaard's Religiousness A. Through the progressive steps of resignation, suffering and guilt a person's relationship to "an eternal happiness" is defined and Religiousness A is attained. Miguel de Unamuno advocates for the kind of resignation that Kierkegaard calls for when he passionately desires immortality and relates all else to that absolute. Unamuno sees that there is no meaning in this life if it ends in death. He recognizes that desiring to live on through one's children or one's work are false goals that make a mockery of immortality. At the end of *Del sentimiento trágico de la vida* he says:

> Hay que creer en la otra vida, en la vida eterna de más allá de la tumba, y en una vida individual y personal, en una vida en que cada uno de nosotros sienta su conciencia y la sienta unirse, sin confundirse, con las demás conciencias todas en la Conciencia Suprema, en Dios; hay que creer en esa otra vida para poder vivir ésta y soportarla y darle sentido y finalidad. Y hay que creer acaso en esa otra vida para merecerla, para conseguirla, o tal vez ni la merece ni la consigue el que no la anhela sobre la razón, y si fuere menester, hasta contra ella. (7:261)

> (One must believe in the other life, in eternal life beyond the tomb, in a life that is individual and personal, in a life in which each one of us feels his consciousness and feels it united, without confusing

> it with all the other consciousnesses in the Supreme Conscious-
> ness, in God; one must believe in that other life in order to be able
> to live in this one and to put up with it, and to give it sense and
> finality. And one must believe in that other life, perhaps, in order
> to merit it, to obtain it, for it may be that he neither merits it nor
> will obtain it who does not passionately desire it above reason and,
> if need be, against reason.)

The proof of his profound desire to live eternally will be seen in his own
conduct as he seeks to live as though he merited eternal life (7:264).

Suffering, the second of Kierkegaard's steps in Religiousness A, is a
central part of Unamuno's faith. He thoroughly understands the suffering
that is caused when the longing for the eternal life that gives this life meaning must be embraced in the face of rationality. Reason and the passions
of the heart will always be in tension and will always result in suffering.
Unamuno understands that the attainment of immortality is necessarily
dependent on God, though the proof of such a God is impossible. Declar-
ing that wanting to believe that God exists is enough, he chooses to live as
though God exists, accepting the suffering that the struggle to know produces and the fact that the question is never resolved.

Though Unamuno does not seem to fulfill the third step of Religiousness A, to accept the need for God to provide the solution for personal guilt,
I believe that his full embrace of the first two steps situates him firmly in
Religiousness A. Climacus has a deep appreciation for this stage of existence.
He says, "Religiousness A . . . is so strenuous for a human being that there is
always a sufficient task in it" (CUP 557). He later adds, "A person existing religiously can express his relation to an eternal happiness (immortality, eternal
life) outside Christianity, and it certainly has also been done, since it must
be said of Religiousness A that even if it had not been present in paganism
it could have been" (CUP 559). Unamuno's faith functions outside the para-
digm of orthodox Christianity, but its central requirements are consonant
with Religoiusness A and as such are religiously profound and demanding.

We can now understand better how it is that none of the kinds of
Christianity whether Catholic or Lutheran or Liberal Protestant, mentioned in the religious labels at the beginning of this book captures the
thought of Miguel de Unamuno; we can also see that the critics who call
Unamuno an atheist are far off the mark. If we understand Unamuno's faith
as the faith found in Religiousness A, we see that his faith is one that includes the ethical sphere of existence that recognizes commitments that are

required by a force beyond oneself. It is a faith that requires "an absolute relation to the absolute" as Unamuno resigns all to embrace the problem of immortality. It is a faith that is willing to suffer, to make of life a struggle for the truth, even though one may never know the truth about what happens after death. Unamuno's faith is his lived philosophy, and in Kierkegaardian terms it is "strenuous" and provides Unamuno with a "sufficient task" for a lifetime. We now turn to the specific ways in which Unamuno took up the task and lived out his faith.

8

Conclusion

How Miguel de Unamuno Lived Out His Faith

IT IS WHOLLY APPROPRIATE that we end this study of Unamuno's quest for faith with the practical results of his faith in his life. We saw some of the historically marked events of his life in chapter 2 as we sketched how those events affected Unamuno's spiritual formation. Coming full circle now, I want to revisit the chronology of Unamuno's life to specifically highlight those actions that stemmed from his deeply seated beliefs. The following is a brief summary of the substance of the previous chapters outlining what those beliefs are: 1) truth must be lived, 2) the most important truth that confronts us is our death, 3) we live in perpetual struggle because there is no easy answer to the longing for immortality since God's existence is unknowable and 4) accepting that suffering and doubt are integral to the struggle, one must live one's life as though God existed, believing in a life after this one.

Unamuno invited scrutiny of his own life when he said that his own conduct should be the proof of his passionate desire for immortality. His ethical challenge to his reader is: "Obra de modo que merezcas a tu propio juicio y a juicio de los demás la eternidad, que te hagas insustituible, que no merezcas morir" (8:264). ("Work as though you merit eternal life, by your own judgment and the judgment of others; make yourself irreplaceable, as though you do not deserve to die.") By being irreplaceable Unamuno means to emphasize that we are each unique and that our occupation becomes our vocation, so that we work with religious significance no matter what the job. He gives the example of a shoemaker who does not do his work just to make a living, just to keep his customers coming back, but rather one who does his job for the love of God and for his desire for eternity, doing his job so well that he makes himself indispensable. Such a person's loss is real when he dies.

Unamuno believed that it was his responsibility to awaken the Spanish people to the reality of death and their need to struggle with the inevitability of the end of life in order to make this life meaningful. This was his calling, his way of meriting eternal life. "Me atrevo a decir que es mi anhelo de vivir y de vivir por siempre el que me inspira esas doctrinas. Y si con ellas logro corroborar y sostener en otro ese mismo anhelo, acaso desfalleciente, habré hecho obra humana y, sobre todo, habré vivido" (7:186). ("I dare to say that it is my longing to live, to live always, which inspires these doctrines within me. And if with them I succeed in corroborating or sustaining that same longing in another person, even if it had been dead, I will have achieved a humane work, and above all, I will have lived.")

To be able to tell the story of how Unamuno lived out his faith, I will again rely largely on the biography of Unamuno titled simply, *Miguel de Unamuno: Biografía*, by French professors Colettte and Jean-Claude Rabaté. The Rabatés have given the reader of Unamuno an unparalleled, detailed vision of the life of the author that demonstrates Unamuno's commitment to liberal ideals, even if his rhetoric was inflammatory and the result was not always successful. By liberal I mean the most expansive and generous sense of that word that includes support for the dignity of the individual, freedom of conscience and freedom of expression. By fighting for the liberal cause in word and deed Unamuno can be said to have lived out his philosophy of making himself irreplaceable, making his unmistakable mark on Spanish society.

It was mentioned in chapter 2 that the overwhelming image of Unamuno that one receives in the Rabatés' narrative is that of the political Unamuno. Though Unamuno's self-sacrificing commitment to liberal ideals is brought to light in new ways with astonishing detail, one is left with the sense that there must be much more to the story. Unamuno's struggle with immortality and his desire to awaken his reader to that defining problem throughout his life and his literary corpus are barely mentioned. His penchant for stirring up controversy is recorded, but there is no attempt to give a comprehensive theory behind the actions of the philosopher except in the matter of his political endeavors. I believe that a fuller picture of the man is found through seeing his political passions, his dedication to liberal principles, as an outgrowth of his faith. As we shall see, even his commitment to socialism was connected to his desire that the individual have the real opportunity to contemplate his own end and struggle with his destiny.

Unamuno's dedication to the individual is grounded in his faith. Rejecting materialism when he speaks about immortality, what he values is the individual consciousness surviving death in some way. As we saw earlier, he is not interested in theories that claim that no energy is lost in the cosmos and that we all return to some undifferentiated mass when we die. He wants his own individual substance to live on, and in struggling to make sense of his own immortality he wants to prod every individual to enter into that struggle. From the start Unamuno articulated his interest in the individual, "Nunca he sentido el deseo de conmover a una muchedumbre y de influir sobre una masa de personas—que pierden su personalidad al amasarse—, yo he sentido, en cambio, siempre furioso anhelo de inquietar el corazón de cada hombre y de influir sobre cada uno de mis hermanos en humanidad. Cuando he hablado en público he procurado casi siempre hacer oratoria lírica, y me he esforzado por forjarme la ilusión de que hablaba a uno solo de mis oyentes, a uno cualquiera, a cualquiera de ellos, a cada uno, no a todos en conjunto" (1:1255). ("I have never felt a desire to move a crowd of people or to influence a mass of people who lose their personality by being part of the crowd. I have felt, on the other hand, a furious longing to disquiet the heart of each man and to influence each one of my brothers in humanity. When I have spoken in public, I have almost always endeavored to produce lyric oratory, and I have tried to form for myself the illusion that I was talking with only one of my hearers, to any one of them, to each one, not to all of them together.")

Unamuno's desire is to awaken the hearts of each of his brothers because they all share the same need to live on in their individual consciousness through the Supreme Consciousness of God. His brothers included the rich, the poor, the intellectual, the farmer and the laborer. He would not have gone out of his way, as we do now, to include his "sisters" in this statement, but as we will see, he defended the rights of women as well. Unamuno's commitment to the individual is what drove his championing of liberal views, and it did so very early in his life.

In the first chapter of the Rabatés' *Miguel de Unamuno* we learn of the fifteen year old's first published article, one that advocated the union of the Basque-Navarro parties to support the *fueros*, local laws that helped to define the Basque identity. Unamuno later characterized his own zeal as sentimentalism for a Basque legend that was more romantic than real. The first publication is important for Unamuno's rejection of its thesis in 1885 when he articulated his fundamentally liberal stance in this way: "Odio todo lo que huele a partido, a escuela o a secta, porque nunca he podido persuadirme que no sea un necio el hombre que profesa integras todas las doctrinas de un partido, secta o escuela y rechaza las demás . . . La sociedad humana debe basarse sobre el individuo particular humano, sobre la personalidad concreta y no la abstracta."[1] ("I hate everything that smells of being partisan, a school or a sect, because I have never been able to persuade myself that the man who wholly believes all of the doctrines of a party, a sect or a school and rejects all the rest isn't a fool . . . . Human society should base itself on the particular human individual, on the concrete personality and not on the abstract.")

Unamuno's relationship with his native city of Bilbao and the Basque identity was fraught with difficulty as he distanced himself from what he saw was more legend than fact in the history of the language and the people. However, he was clear in saying that his socialist roots were formed by observation of the rise of capitalism in the Basque province and the exploitation of workers that produced the material wealth for the owners. His socialist thought was more formed by Henry George than Karl Marx, and his sympathies lay with the workers and their unions. He saw socialism as the antidote to anarchism and the radical individualism of the bourgeoisie. Though he was willing to write for *La Lucha de Clases* and declare himself to be a socialist in print, he was neither a militant Marxist nor a materialist. Of course, his nuanced positions were lost on the conservatives, those who wanted to protect private property as well as those religious figures who saw his views as dangerous for the young students whom he was teaching.

In the political polemics surrounding the foundation of the Basque identity and the growing problems of industrialization, Unamuno's concern is with the individual. The young author became a member of the liberal group El Sitio as early as 1885, a group that was formed to honor those who fought against the Carlists in a civil war that the child Unamuno experienced first-hand. Even so, he was unwilling to mouth the party line with regard to the history of the Basque people which he had already declared "unscientific" in his doctoral dissertation. With regard to the warring parties extant in the Basque political scene, one that looked to the past and one that looked to the future, Unamuno took no stance. Rather he said, "pedid el reino de la libertad, de la libertad individual y todo lo demás se os dará

---

1. Unamuno, quoted in Rabaté and Rabaté, *Miguel de Unamuno*, 83.

por añadidura" rewriting a bit of scripture (4:174). ("ask for the kingdom of liberty, of the kingdom of the freedom of the individual, and all the rest will be added to you.")

The increasing problems of a capitalistic society in which the bourgeoisie profited from cheap labor were manifest as there were growing strikes of miners in Nervión and Vizcaya. Unamuno's sympathies are clearly with the miners whom he sees as exploited slaves. He writes to a friend, "V. sabe lo que son las minas, cuatro millonarios explotando vilmente a un rebaño de esclavos. Todo el mundo (menos los dueños) clama por los mineros, víctimas de una explotación inicua."[2] ("You know what the mines are, four millionaires vilely exploiting a sheep herd of slaves. Everyone (except the owners) cries out on behalf of the miners, victims of iniquitous exploitation.") By 1890 Unamuno was expressing his socialist views in print, participating in the surge of socialist activism in and around Bilbao.

In 1891 Unamuno competed for and finally received a position to teach Greek at the University of Salamanca, moving there in July of that year. Very soon he acquired a reputation for being the young rebel professor who at the age of twenty-seven already stood out from the rest of the fifty *catedráticos,* (tenured professors) whose average age was forty-nine. Already in September of 1891 he was writing for *La Libertad,* a periodical of Salamanca that was willing to publish Unamuno's criticism of the monarchy, considering it a form of government whose time had long past, advocating instead the participation of all Spaniards, which the Rabatés characterize as a further articulation of Unamuno's stance for universal suffrage.[3]

Unamuno began to collaborate with the journal *La Lucha de Clases* with a famous declaration of his faith in socialism in October of 1894, though he was wary of identifying himself with any doctrinaire group, saying of such groups, "Ellos ponen las ideas sobre las personas y yo las personas sobre las ideas."[4] ("They put ideas over people and I put people over ideas.") Quickly it became clear that Unamuno was not following the party line, was not a Marxist materialist and was impatient with the divide between what he called manual workers and intellectual workers. Unamuno explained the socialism that he was advocating to Clarín: "Sueño con que el socialismo sea una verdadera reforma religiosa cuando se marchite el dogmatismo marxiano y se vea algo más que lo puramente económico.

2. Ibid., 90.

3. Rabaté and Rabaté, *Unamuno,* 121.

4. Unamuno, quoted in Rabaté and Rabaté, *Unamuno,* 147.

¡Qué tristeza el ver lo que se llama socialismo! ¡Qué falta de fe en el progreso, y qué falta de humanidad!"[5] ("I dream of socialism that it will be a real religious reform when the Marxist dogmatism fades and it is seen as something that is more than purely economic. How sad to see what is called socialism! What a lack of faith in progress and what a lack of humanity!") Here we have the integration of Unamuno's political and religious views, one affecting the other in lived consequences.

But Unamuno's expansive views on what socialism is did not sit well with the purists that wrote for *La Lucha de Clases*, and there was a falling out with the leadership there. Unamuno lived his anti-dogma stance by writing an article that called for all stripes of socialists to come and work together, including Christians, both Catholic and Protestant, as well as trade unionists. His view was that these sorts of folks were after justice, but the powers that be in the party were not in agreement with letting such people in and the divide between the manual laborers and the intellectuals grew.

In chapter 2 we saw the effect on Unamuno of the illness of his son, Raimundo, whose hydrocephalic condition worsened and seemed incurable by 1896. Soon after the night in March of 1897 when Unamuno experienced overwhelming anxiety coupled with the physical symptoms of a heart attack, he wrote to his friend Leopoldo Gutiérrez Abascal that even in his present state of angst with family and personal problems, he still considered himself a socialist. Why, in this moment, would Unamuno bring up the political? For this philosopher, the socialism that he advocated would practically affect the ability of people to confront the most important question, the question of immortality. He wrote that the goal of socialism was, "el procurar bienestar temporal a todos y emancipación es para que, libres de la cadena de las necesidades absorbentes, despierten del sueño y vean la vida a la luz de la muerte."[6] ("to procure the temporal well-being of everyone and emancipation so that, free from the chain of absorbing necessities, they can wake from the dream and see life in the light of death.") One is not surprised to read that Unamuno's fellow socialists were not at all amused at news of the new religious bent that Don Miguel had taken, given that their doctrinaire socialism excluded faith and anyone who professed it. But if they had understood Unamuno's views, they would have seen his socialism and his renewed interest in religious questions as perfectly compatible. Later Unamuno wrote to the same friend that in his socialism he wanted

5 Alas, *Epistolario a Clarín*, 53.

6. Unamuno, quoted in Rabaté and Rabaté, *Unamuno*, 163.

to assure that the foundation of social progress be "del verdadero progreso individual, de la ascensión a Dios por Cristo," ("the true progress of the individual, the ascension to God through Christ,") and that he felt, "más socialista cuanto más cristiano."[7] ("more socialist the more Christian.")

Unamuno was willing to put his position and prestige at the service of justice, not just theoretically but practically and personally. On Corpus Christi day in 1896 there was a bombing during religious processions for the occasion in Barcelona. At least 12 people were killed and there were many injuries. The attack was said to be the responsibility of anarchists. The government, in an attempt to squelch the anarchist movement once and for all, rounded up hundreds of supposed anarchists and put them on trial in a military court that received the name El Proceso de Montjuich. There was no proof for the conviction of these men, so the government tortured many of them to get "confessions." Among those detained and tried was Pere Corominas, one of the editors of *Ciencia Social,* a journal devoted to intellectual anarchist thought, and a friend of Unamuno. Unamuno headed the efforts of a group of intellectuals that included Leopoldo Alas, Clarín, and Francisco Giner de los Ríos in defending the prisoners of Montjuich, their treatment and the entire sham of the trial. Unamuno went so far as to write to the president of the government, Antonio Cánovas del Castillo, pleading for his friend Pere Corominas, saying that he was no more culpable than himself in this tragic event. Unamuno received a reply from the president saying that he would look into the situation. The efforts of the defenders had some effect, but not entirely what they had hoped. In December of 1896 Corominas was sentenced to eight years and eight months in prison. Unamuno continued to advocate for his friend. In May of 1897 five of the accused were executed, others were given sentences for life or less, others, like Pere Corominas, were pardoned but exiled.

At the same time that Unamuno was writing publically and personally on his friend's behalf, the press was full of the conflict in Cuba. Unamuno believed that the will of the island peoples should determine their destiny and he wrote against the military effort of the Spanish government there. He saw the conflict as no more justified than that of archaic duels between persons whose honor had somehow been besmirched. Unamuno saw his ideal socialism as an antidote to war. He wrote, "Frente a la política de razas, de naciones, de regiones, frente a las estupideces y miserias del proteccionismo, . . . debe promover el Socialismo el más amplio cosmopolitismo, el

7. Ibid., 169 and 172.

más absoluto librecambio, la movilización mayor posible del obrero."[8] ("In face of the policy of racism, of nations, of regions, in face of the stupidities and miseries of protectionism, . . . socialism should promote a more ample cosmopolitanism, the most absolute interchange, the largest mobilization of the worker possible.") Of course, the island did gain its independence from Spain along with Puerto Rico and the Philippines after the defeat of the Spanish navy in July of 1898.

Unamuno extended to women the right of people to determine their own destiny. It would be difficult to characterize Unamuno as a feminist in the contemporary sense of the word, but there are evidences of his respect for women, not the least of which was his relationship with his wife, Concha, who seemed to be the stabilizing force in his life for all of their faithful, married years. While she bore him nine children, whom he loved without bound, she was his anchor in all of the ups and downs of his rectorship at the University of Salamanca and the political and ecclesiastical machinations against him. He said of her that he owed to her, "todo lo que en él valga,"[9] ("all that was of any worth in him.") Concha also read his manuscripts and during the time of Unamuno's exile he entrusted to her the oversight of all of the translations of his works that were in process in Germany and Italy. While Unamuno depreciated the taste of women from time to time, he did so in the context of their not knowing better. He advocated for the education of women that had not been widely available to those unable to pay for it. In August of 1906 he gave lectures at the Instituto de Málaga in which he called for educational systems to be formative for men, women and children. He was critical of the education of children, as he had been since his own forays into organized education, expressed in *Recuerdos de niñez*. There he spoke of teachers that were tyrants and the rigid, narrowness of the subject matter. Even for children Unamuno advocated "una escuela de libertad y de dignidad humana," ("a school of freedom and human dignity") and he says that love for the student must be the motivation for every teacher.[10]

Another of the causes about which Unamuno spoke and wrote often was the matter of agrarian reform. He decried the fact that so much of the land was controlled by so few. He saw the agrarian problem as the cause of emigration from Spain to the Americas which continued to be a drain on

8. Ereño Altuna, *Artículos inéditos en La Lucha de Clases,* 175.

9. Unamuno, quoted in Rabaté and Rabaté, *Unamuno,* 266–67.

10. Ibid., 263.

Spanish resources into the twentieth century. When in 1912 José Canalejas Méndez, the president of the Consejo de Ministros was assassinated by an anarchist, Manuel Pardiñas Serrano, Unamuno blamed the rich for his murder, those land holders who dealt with their tenants unjustly and the ministers of religion who supported them. Since Canalejas was a lone advocate of agrarian justice, Unamuno blamed his assassination on the fact that, "no haya en España verdadero partido liberal democrático, es más, que no haya un verdadero liberalism."[11] ("there is no true liberal, democratic party in Spain, and even more, there is no true liberalism.") In the spring of 1914 he continued with his *campaña agraria* denouncing the great property owners who were so absent from their lands that they could not recognize wheat when it was harvested or a sheep from a goat (7:561).

As we saw in chapter 2, Unamuno paid dearly for his advocacy on the part of the laborer, whether that be for industrial workers in Bilbao or tillers of the earth in Castilla, when he was dismissed from his post as rector of the University of Salamanca in August of 1914. He was never given reasons for his removal or a chance to defend himself. Unamuno knew that there could be no cause to remove him from his office on the basis of inattention to the details of administration or the lack of eminence of his scholarship. He surmised that his fate had been caused by his widely distributed support of agrarian reform, for his arguments with the Jesuits, and for his socialist views expressed in so many journals of the day.

At almost the same time as his dismissal from his post as rector, the rest of the world was plunged into war. Spain declared its neutrality early, but the sympathies of the government, the church and the monarchy lay with the Germans, admiring their discipline and their ability to keep order. The intellectuals along with the laborers and the socialists all declared themselves on the side of the Allied Forces, and Unamuno was among the most vocal of its defenders. He had written against German aggression and materialism before the beginning of the war, but he became very critical in the press and along with many other intellectuals signed the Manifiesto de la Liga Antigermanófila (Manifesto of the Anti-German League) in January of 1917. He also welcomed the entrance of the United States into the hostilities and continued to speak publically against Spain's neutral stance in the war. After one such speech the newspaper *El País* opined that Unamuno's "burning convictions" with regard to the war had help to clear up other

---

11 Unamuno, *De patriotismo espiritual*, 305.

contradictions and confusions in his mind.[12] When the war ended, Unamuno was one of the first to sign a manifesto asking that Spain be part of the League of Nations, but in the manifesto the signatories recognized that to be part of such a society of free nations, Spain needed to be democratized because the government of the present Spain was far from a democracy. Unfortunately, by 1919 Unamuno saw that the opposite had happened in Spain. Unamuno wrote that while Germany had been defeated, its legacy in Spain had won.[13]

Unamuno had long criticized the king, Alfonso XIII, on many fronts but especially for being ineffectual and choosing the worst of ministers. He took as a personal affront the fact that he had requested an interview with the king as early 1915, but he had never received a response. In 1922 Unamuno was conceded an audience with the king where he was said to have put forth his point of view with no less force than ever, but he was criticized by some for even being present with the monarch. By 1923 the dictator Miguel Primo de Rivera had brought about a military coup that suspended constitutional guarantees. Some intellectuals were taken in by the dictator, but not Unamuno who saw the man as vacuous and stupid.[14] But the personal stupidity of the dictator was not as important as the political tragedy he was bringing about. Later Unamuno wrote, "Dictar dogmas es matar la libertad de la inteligencia, es matar la inteligencia, porque la inteligencia es libertad. Entender es lo único que liberta. La obediencia ciega, propia del esclavo, no es de hombres (8:514). ("To pronounce dogmas is to kill the freedom of intelligence because intelligence is freedom. To understand is the only thing that liberates. Blind obedience is appropriate for a slave but not for a man.") What Unamuno published in print was more subject to censorship day by day. His criticism of the regime and its censorship needed to be published outside of Spain and therefore made its way to the Argentinian newspaper, *La Nación,* through which he developed a large following in that part of the world.

As we saw in chapter 2, for his relentless criticism of the dictator and the king, Unamuno was officially exiled from the country in February of 1924, stripped of his position and his salary. The reaction of the Catholic press was predictable: the government was quite justified in ridding the country of this man who did not respect divine or civil law. The reaction

12. Rabaté and Rabaté, *Unamuno,* 370.
13. Ibid., 392.
14. Ibid., 443.

of students was equally predictable; they took to the streets in protest. In Fuerteventura Unamuno received notice of newspapers in France and Argentina protesting his exile and denouncing the Spanish government. The censors were so vigilant in Spain that they opened his letters to his friends, and even though *La Nación* in Argentina had editorialized against the Spanish government on Unamuno's behalf, they began to be skittish about publishing his own harsh diatribes against the Spanish state there. But Unamuno was adamant about not asking for pardon from the regime for transgressions that he had not committed. He commended the safekeeping of his wife and younger children to the three children that were then making their own living as well as to friends, of which there were many.

Though word of an amnesty offered by the government reached Unamuno on July 5, 1924, he and his fellow exile Rodrigo Soriano rejected the amnesty saying that they neither believed it nor trusted the conduct of those who offered it. They considered their situation to be very dangerous and would not return to Spain until Spain was a much different country. Even as he was fleeing from Las Palmas to Paris, on a stop in Lisbon he gave the following statement to a local newspaper:"Hoy en España, la mejor esperanza de regeneración está en el partido socialista obrero, el más humano y por lo tanto, el más patriótico y el que ha defendido la civilidad."[15] ("Today in Spain, the best hope of regeneration is found in the socialist workers' party, the most humane and therefore the most patriotic party and the one that has defended civility.") This he wrote on his journey to France, arranged and paid for by the French government, a country that Unamuno saw as one that upheld the civil rights of all people.

Unamuno was well received in Paris, but he tired of life there fairly quickly. The turbulent state of his inner self during this time can be found in *La agonía del cristianismo,* published first in France. He decided to be a thorn in the literal side of the Spanish government by taking up residence in the far southwestern city of Hendaya, France, just across the border from Irún, Spain. He was also received well there by the president of the Liga de los Derechos del Hombre (League of the Rights of Man). Unamuno was led to believe through intermediaries that he could return to Spain if he would just quiet his voice and his pen, which he was not willing to do.

From Hendaya Unamuno heard about the proceedings to fill his position as professor of Greek at the University of Salamanca. The post was given to a priest who was said to be woefully ignorant of Greek and of

15. Urrutia León, *Miguel de Unamuno desconocido*, 213.

much else. When a group of professors and students protested the decision outside of the room where it was taken, four of the students were arrested. The esteemed Junta Directiva (Executive Board) of the Ateneo de Madrid protested the arrests which they all signed, denouncing the Spanish Army for not allowing the intellectuals the liberty of thought. The manifesto was not allowed to be published in Spain, but it was published in the Latin American press. Though Unamuno might have written about his disgust for the ridiculous appointment of one so unqualified for his position, or he might have written to defend those who were unlawfully arrested in his support, Unamuno took on the writers of the manifesto saying, "no se debe hablar en nombre de la intelectualidad, sino de la moralidad, de la hombría de bien y pedir, no un mínimum de libertad sino pura justicia."[16] ("One should not speak in the name of intellectuality but in the name of morality, of integrity and ask not a minimum of freedom, but rather, pure justice." He ended with his own manifesto, "Un sagrado deber de patria y de humanidad nos manda oponernos a los tiranos y verdugos de España."[17] ("A sacred obligation of the fatherland and of humanity demands that we oppose the tyrants and the executioners of Spain.")

There is no doubt that the family suffered a great deal in Unamuno's absence, though the older children were out and making a living on their own. Even so, Concha supported her husband in what he was doing and agreed never to ask for any pardon or any concession on his behalf. After one visit that Concha, son Fernando and daughter Salome had made to Hendaya to visit Unamuno during the Christmas holidays, Concha was detained by the police. She was actually put into jail for several hours upon returning to Spain through Irún for carrying with her four copies of *Hojas Libres*, a journal whose purpose was to protest against the dictatorship of Primo de Rivera and Alfonso XIII, published by Eduardo Ortega y Gasset, and with which Unamuno collaborated. Concha later reported that she was in jail long enough to offer to help some of the prisoners mend their clothes, but she was allowed to leave without her passport before she could finish the work. *Hojas Libres* was smuggled into Spain from Hendaya regularly, and Unamuno dedicated an entire article to his wife's steadfastness in a subsequent issue of the journal.

Unamuno was aware of the activity of kindred spirits in other countries of Europe, and added his voice to their protest against tyranny. In

16. Unamuno, quoted in Rabaté and Rabaté, *Unamuno*, 515.
17. Ibid., 516.

October of 1928 he signed a manifesto with other exiled persons, among them an Italian, Cipriano Facciometti which was published in Italy and smuggled into Spain in *Hojas Libres*. Unamuno was cognizant of an Antifascist International Congress that was going to take place in Berlin, and though he would not leave Hendaya to attend, he asked that an open letter he had written to the assembled participants be translated and that the head of the delegation from Spain read it at the Congress.

Unamuno was firm in his resolve not to return to Spain until civil liberties were reinstated. In the waning days of 1929 political change was in the air in Madrid as Primo de Rivera lost the support of the military, the business sector and even the king, who dismissed him and brought in his place General Dámaso Berenguer. At the beginning of 1930 Unamuno learned that his position at the university was to be restored, but he waited until February 9 to reenter the country through a carefully planned itinerary, first to Irún, across the bridge from Hendaya, then to Bilbao, on to Salamanca and finally to Madrid, to the Ateneo. As the Rabatés recount the story, Unamuno's reentry into Spain was dramatic as crowds had gathered on both sides of the bridge. The mayor of Hendaya cried, "¡Viva la libertad!" "Let freedom live!" and embraced him in the middle of the bridge before Unamuno finished the crossing over into Spain.[18] When he got to Irún he gave the following statement to a Republican newspaper in San Sebastián: "Al volver a España, después de seis años de ausencia, . . . espero que asistamos pronto al parto de la civilidad española, al fin de los pronunciamientos y de toda dictadura, sea de reyes, de castas, o de clases. Y al entronizamiento de la justicia que es la libertad de la verdad."[19] ("Upon returning to Spain after six years of absence, I hope that we will soon attend the birth of Spanish civility, to the death of pronouncements, of all sorts of dictatorial rule, be it of kings, or privilege or class. And to the enthronement of justice, which is freedom of the truth.") Almost in cinematographic style, on the 13th of February,1930, Unamuno made his triumphal entry into Salamanca in an entourage of some fifty cars. The crowds that lined the streets made it so difficult for the entourage to move that it took more than an hour to traverse the last two kilometers. After finally reaching his home and greeting his family, Unamuno stepped out on the balcony to address the crowd. He reminded them of what he had said when he left six years earlier, "Volveré no con mi libertad que nada vale, sino

18. Rabaté and Rabaté, *Unamuno*, 548.

19 Unamuno, quoted in Rabaté and Rabaté, *Unamuno*, 548.

con la vuestra."[20] ("I will return, not with my freedom, which does not really matter, but with yours.")

Unamuno took up his old teaching responsibilities and proceeded to publish criticism of the king and of the Spanish intervention in Africa. Though constitutional guarantees had been supposedly reinstated, he found his work censured again. He began to see with many that the Republic would come, and he put his name forward for the April 1930 local elections as part of the Republican/Socialist coalition which was victorious. Unamuno was elected and led a large demonstration in the Plaza Mayor on April 14 in which the flag of the Republic was raised and he declared the triumph of the Republic. On the same day King Alfonso heard of these declarations throughout the land, and he decided to leave the country. The revolutionary committee made sweeping changes immediately. There would be agrarian reform, freedom of worship, and respect for private property. Soon Unamuno was reinstated by his fellow professors as rector of the university once again.

In July of 1931 Unamuno was elected as a senator for the Asamblea Constituyente along with six others from Salamanca in the Conjunción Republicano-Socialista. He took pride in the fact that the Republic had come about as a result of the ballot box and not a military coup. He was welcomed to that body with a standing ovation that he said made him very uncomfortable as no one person should be given more credit or honor in bringing about the Republic. He participated actively in the discussions that finally brought about the Constitution of 1931 in December of that year, including changes in the ability of persons to divorce and a revoking of many privileges for the Church, including the dissolving of the Order of the Jesuits. In writing about the state of the Church in 1932, Unamuno urged the bishops to embrace liberalism rather than reject it because the liberal cause was one that could really rejuvenate the faith. He feared that the Church would continue its attacks on liberalism, though, and he respectfully asked the Church to return to its original mission.[21]

To the youth he said, "Trabajar es orar. El que da con el mazo ruega a Dios. Y Dios le oye. Asentemos una República de hombres libres, responsables y disciplinados, y como decía Cristo, hágase la luz, para que podamos encaminar al fin a esta España por un camino de gloria" (9:426–27). ("To work is to pray. He who strikes with a mallet pleads with God. And God

20. Ibid., 553.
21. Rabaté and Rabaté, *Unamuno*, 592.

hears him. Let us put into place a Republic of free, responsible, disciplined men and as Christ said, be light, so that we can guide Spain to the end to a road of glory.") Unamuno saw the need for God's help, but he did not want one political cause to claim Christ for its cause. He denounced an incipient fascism which he saw in some young people who had taken the cross of Christ for its symbol, calling instead for their support of the liberal, democratic Republic that was the opportunity and challenge of the moment.

Nevertheless, Unamuno bristled at criticism that he did not support the Republic when he disapproved and vocally disagreed with a policy. In his evenhanded way, Unamuno pointed out that the Republic was not an end in itself but rather the means to the end of equality and saving Spain. "Se dice que hay que salvar ante todo la República. Efectivamente; hay que salvarla porque es el medio de salvar a España, pero no como un fin, sino como un medio" (9:443). ("It is said that above all, the Republic must be saved. Effectively, it must be saved because it is the means of saving Spain, not as an end in itself but as a means.") In his participation in the Liga de los Derechos del Hombre (League of Human Rights) he advocated for the protection of the rights of all people, not just the rich and the privileged but of the worker and all who found their rights violated. Once again, this sense of equality was based in Unamuno's foundational belief that each individual must have a consciousness that ultimately derived from the Supreme Consciousness, and that individual consciousness has meaning in this life because of its preservation after death.

In fact, by November of 1932 Unamuno was very disillusioned with the Second Republic and spoke out in the Ateneo in Madrid. He feared that the vote that brought in the Republic was a vote against the monarchy and against the dictator, but it was not a vote of confidence or support for democratic reforms. He saw some of the actions of the Republic as reprisals, such as the dissolution of the Jesuits and the confiscation of their property. He mourned the burning of convents and pointed out the difficulty of finding competent teachers who were not priests. He even found the censorship that was most abhorrent under the dictatorship still to be present. He said that the present liberalism was not the liberalism of real freedom, the sort that he had espoused in his youth. He feared that the rift between the government and the will of the people had grown to an abyss. While he had spoken against the entanglement of the government and the Church in the past, he also declared that the "religión de Estado," "religion of the state," that is, communism and fascism, were just as bad.[22]

During these difficult political times Unamuno's personal trials grew, especially with the illness and impending death of his beloved wife, Concha. She had acquired what was described then as "forgetfulness," which we today would probably call dementia or Alzheimer's disease. Unamuno canceled a trip to France to receive an honorary doctorate because of the precarious nature of Concha's health. Concha died on May 15, 1934 and Unamuno wrote after her passing that she had supported him in his struggles to regain his faith and added, "Se me fue con Dios; me ha dejado su rocío. Y ahora, bajo su mirada eterna, a mi brega ¡a renovarme en ésta y en ella!" (8:1208–1211). ("She left me to be with God; she has left me her dew. And now, under her eternal gaze, to my struggle, to renew myself in it and in her!") Though living through what he himself described as the worst misfortune of his life, Unamuno sought from her memory the inspiration for renewal of his energy for the tasks at hand.

Within a few months, Unamuno retired from the University with great honor. On his seventieth birthday, the 29th of September of 1934 Unamuno was named rector for life of the University of Salamanca. The season of tributes began as the city of Salamanca honored him with the title of perpetual mayor and they reenacted his triumphal entry to the city after his exile. When Unamuno took his place to give his last lecture in the Paraninfo he told his listeners as well as all who would read his published address later, "Tened fe en la palabra, que es cosa vivida; sed hombres de palabra, hombres De Dios, Suprema Cosa y Palabra Suma, y Él nos reconozca a todos como suyos en España" (9:451). ("Have faith in the word, which is a living thing, be men of the word, men of God, Supreme Thing, Supreme Word, and may he recognize all of us as his in Spain.")

The Republic was shown to be more and more unstable daily. There were bloody uprisings and brutal reactions by the Republican government in Cataluña and Asturias. In early 1935 with Ramón Valle-Inclán and many other intellectuals Unamuno signed a petition asking for the death penalty to be abolished as it was used so indiscriminately in the desire for quick retribution. At the same time Unamuno did something that astounded his liberal and Republican friends. At the invitation of José Antonio Primo de Rivera, the son of the dictator who had exiled him, Unamuno attended a meeting of the Spanish Phalange. He was criticized in the press for his

22. Ibid., 606.

presence at the meeting of such a rightest group, but he was living out what he professed when he said, "A nadie, sujeto o partido, grupo, escuela o capilla, le reconozco la autenticidad y menos la exclusividad del patriotismo. En todas sus formas, aun las más opuestas y contradictorias entre sí, en siendo de buena fe y de amor, cabe salvación civil" (9:460). ("In no one person, no subject, or party or group or school or chapel do I recognize authentic, much less exclusivity of patriotism. In all of its forms, even the most opposite and contradictory ones themselves, in being of good faith and love, is found civil salvation.") Unamuno continued to publically denounce the fascist fascination of young people who allowed their brains to be sterilized and who conformed to propaganda too easily, but he did not rule out the possibility of sitting down to dinner with the Phalange to talk civilly about differences.

Unamuno began his last year on this earth, 1936, making a trip to England to receive an honorary degree from Oxford University. In the several speeches given over a number of days Unamuno reflected on his career, the Generation of '98, and his desire throughout all of his writing to awaken the conscience of his fellow countrymen, calling himself an old liberal. But he said that he has stopped speaking in public in Spain (though not writing, of course) because at present no one was listening, just gesticulating.[23] What Unamuno refered to was the two extremes of the political spectrum that were wrenching Spain apart, the anarchists and the fascists. He grew very disturbed upon returning to Spain, and wrote against the barbarity that had come to his country in the newspaper *Ahora*. He opposed the laws that were making education secular, as though education could be neutral, and he saw the Republic as trampling on the traditional faith of the Spanish people.[24] He was willing to put into print his unhappiness with the Republic saying, "Los más de los que votaron la República ni sabían lo que es ella ni sabían lo que iba a ser «esta» República. ¡Que si lo hubiesen sabido!"[25] ("Most of those who voted for the Republic neither knew what it is nor did they know what was going to be 'this' Republic. If they had only known!")

A military commander, Manuel García Álvarez, took over the municipal seat of government in Salamanca along with the post office and the

---

23. Ibid., 659.

24. Colette and Jean-Claude Rabaté add what I would consider an editorial comment when they opine that Unamuno made this criticism about the trampling of faith even though he didn't share that faith. Ibid., 666.

25. Unamuno, quoted in Rabaté and Rabaté, *Unamuno*, 667.

telephone company in a Sunday coup that found Unamuno unwittingly seen as a supporter of the rebellion because he was present in the Plaza Mayor for his morning coffee, as always. The Phalangists had taken power, and at the same time took away Unamuno's ability to write for the national press. He was brought to the City Hall for a ceremony in which he pledged to continue to fight for Spain. His words were taken as an act of treason by one of his friends who learned of them from a jail cell. The same friend was assassinated by the Phalangists some days later. The death of his friend was a terrible shock to Unamuno.[26]

Though Unamuno was unable to write for the national press, the foreign press came to interview him. An anti-marxist newspaper in France declared that Unamuno supported the Nationalist cause. An American reporter revealed in *El Adelanto* that Unamuno had said, "Azaña (the prime minister) debiera suicidarse como acto patriótico," ("Azaña [the prime minister] should commit suicide as a patriotic act.") but Unamuno also added, "Yo no estoy a la derecha ni a la izquierda. Yo no he cambiado. Es el régimen de Madrid el que ha cambiado. Cuando todo pase, estoy seguro de que yo, como siempre, me enfrentaré con los vencedores."[27] ("I am not of the right or of the left. I have not changed. It is the regime in Madrid that has changed. When all of this has passed, I am sure that I, as always, will have my confrontation with the winners.") With Unamuno's prominence, the Republican government did not ignore such a stance and in reprisal, stripped Unamuno of his position as rector for life of the University of Salamanca on August 22, 1936. Once Franco was in place as the Jefe del Gobierno de la Nación (Head of the Government of the Nation) and took over Burgos at the beginning of October, Unamuno was put back in his position as rector, only to lose the position once again as a result of the events of the now infamous Día de la Raza, October 12, celebration of the opening of the school year in the Paraninfo of the University.

By this date it had been duly reported in the newspapers that Unamuno had contributed 5,000 pesetas to the Nationalist cause. Nevertheless, when the proceedings of the opening session became entirely partisan on the fascist side, and the third speaker, Francisco Maldonado, called the Basque Country and Cataluña "cancers" on the body of Spain, Unamuno could not keep from responding: "Se ha hablado de Guerra internacional en defensa de la civilización cristiana occidental; una civilización que yo

26. Rabaté and Rabaté, *Unamuno*, 673.
27. Unamuno, quoted in Rabaté and Rabaté, *Unamuno*, 674.

mismo he defendido otras veces. Pero la de hoy es sólo una guerra incivil. No la guerra civil que de niño viví con el bombardeo de mi Bilbao, una guerra doméstica. Conquistar no es convertir. Vencer no es convencer y no puede convencer el odio que no deja lugar para la compasión; no puede convencer el odio a la inteligencia que es crítica y diferenciadora, inquisitiva y no de inquisición."[28] ("International War in defense of western civilization has been spoken of, and I too have defended it on occasion. But today's war is only an uncivil war. It is not the civil war that I lived as a child with the siege of my Bilbao, a domestic war. To conquer is not to convert. To defeat is not to convince, and hate that does not leave room for compassion cannot convince; hate cannot convince the intelligence, which is critical and differentiating, inquisitive but not the inquisition.)

This recreation of Unamuno's speech is fashioned by the Rabatés from the notes which Unamuno wrote on an envelope which he had in his pocket that day, an envelope that is still extant. It was the envelope containing a letter from the wife of Atilano Coco, the Protestant pastor who had been detained by Francoist forces. In it Doña Enriqueta told Unamuno that her husband had been accused of being a Mason, and she asked for his further intervention.

There is no official transcript of Unamuno's words on that day, even though *La Gaceta Regional* published the speeches of the other speakers; Unamuno's words were censored. Nevertheless, the same newspaper admitted that the entire proceedings were heard by thousands of people in Salamanca and around the country through radio. So what happened and what was said after Unamuno started down this road of severe criticism of the Nationalist cause has been recreated by many different people over the years. The Rabatés and Salcedo include in their accounts at this point the intervention of Franco's General Millán Astray who was incensed by Unamuno and who had tried to take over the meeting, asking if he could speak. Unamuno continued speaking, not relinquishing the podium until Millán Astray began to whip the assembled into shouts of "¡Muera la intelectualidad traidora!" (Death to traitorous intellectuality!") along with "¡Abajo los intelectuales!" ("Down with the intellectuals!") and "¡Viva la muerte.!"[29] ("Long live death!") Unamuno's life is said to have been in danger at this moment as the partisan Nationalist audience reacted indignantly to Unamuno's rhetoric. Some say that were it not for the fact that Unamuno

---

28. Ibid., 685.

29. Ibid., and Salcedo, *Vida de don Miguel*, 415.

was led from the chamber on the arm of Franco's wife, Carmen Polo, the crowd might have brought bodily harm to the elderly man.

For his forthright denunciation of the excesses of power that he saw around him, Unamuno was put under house arrest. The next day his title as honorary mayor of Salamanca was taken away from him, and he was expelled from the advisory council. On the 14th of October his rectorship was taken from him once again by his own colleagues at the University. Unamuno died in his home on the last day of 1936. As the Rabatés point out, he was abandoned by his Republican friends who did not understand how he allowed himself to be swept up in the Nationalist cause, and he was effectively incarcerated by the Nationalist cause, which had attempted to use him for their own ends.[30]

From this writer's point of view, the whole of Unamuno's living out of his philosophy, of giving voice to the liberal cause and defending it whenever and wherever he could, should not be tainted with the fact that his coffin was draped with the Nationalist flag. The presence of the envelope containing the letter from the Protestant pastor's wife in Unamuno's pocket on that fateful day of October 12, 1936 is testimony to his being consistent in his support of human rights, of the freedom of speech and the freedom of religion, until the very end of his life. Unamuno's influence on the political and literary history of Spain was his way of incarnating his desire to live as though there were a God, as though there were an eternal life after this one.

Our point of departure for this study of Unamuno's quest for faith was his own demand that for a philosopher to be worthy of the name, his philosophy must affect the way in which he lived, and we can add by extension, that it must be possible for that philosophy to affect how his followers live their lives. Unamuno claims with Kierkegaard that truth must be lived. The truth of the inevitability of the end of life motivated him to suffer and struggle with doubt, to live with the wound always open and never healed. Unamuno wanted to believe and though he never could reasonably know that God existed, he ordered his life to live as though God existed. The truth of bodily death motivated him to live his life so as to merit eternal life, to make himself irreplaceable. While Unamuno seemed to be in constant conflict with the powers that be, waging war in peace and peace in war, through it all he was defending human rights, freedom from censorship, separation of church and state, agrarian reform, the right to organize unions, the right to vote for people of all classes, the right to denounce abuse of power, in

30. Rabaté and Rabaté, *Unamuno,* 689.

whatever political form that it took. All this he did in the context of his quest for faith, born out in his defense of the individual whose consciousness should be sustained by the consciousness of God. His life is a passionate incarnation of the truth which he espoused. There can be no doubt that he was a philosopher for whom it can be said that he lived what he taught and what he believed.

Why read Unamuno? Why should anyone care about his beliefs and his faith commitments? Because Unamuno challenges his individual reader to take stock of his or her life and calls us all to live our lives meaningfully, facing the fact of our death unflinchingly. His insistence on the contradictions being held in tension and sustaining the struggle may not be persuasive or attractive to many, but his life was a model of authentic existence, with engaged, deliberate attempts to put his faith into action in service of his university, his country and the world. His philosophy and his quest for faith are instructive for any person who cares about existence and living beyond the demands of the day toward a higher calling. He pokes and prods and makes one uncomfortable, even irritating the reader from time to time. But in reacting and responding to his ideas, we have the opportunity to clarify the truth that we can ultimately live.

Bibliography

Alas, Adolfo. *Epistolario a Clarín, Marcelino Menéndez y Pelayo, Miguel de Unamuno, Armando Palacio Valdés,* Madrid, Edición Escorial, 1941.

Baker, Armand. "The God of Unamuno." *Hispania,* 74.4 (December, 1991): 824–33.

Blanco Aguinaga, Carlos. *El Unamuno contemplativo.* México: Nueva Revista de Filología Hispánica, 1959.

Booth, Wayne. *Critical Understanding: The Powers and Limits of Pluralism.* Chicago: University of Chicago Press, 1979.

———. *The Rhetoric of Fiction.* 2nd Edition. Chicago: University of Chicago Press, 1983.

Cerezo Galán, Pedro. *El mal del siglo: El conflicto entre Ilustración y Romanticismo en la crisis finisecular del siglo XIX.* Madrid: Editorial Biblioteca Nueva, 2003.

———. *Las máscaras de lo trágico: Filosofía y tragedia en Miguel de Unamuno.* Madrid: Editorial Trotta, 1996.

Collado, Jesús-Antonio. *Kierkegaard y Unamuno: La existencia religiosa.* Madrid: Editorial Gredos, 1962.

Curtis, Heather. *Faith in the Great Physician: Suffering and Divine Healing in American Culture, 1860–1900.* Baltimore, MD: Johns Hopkins University Press, 2007.

Ereño Altuna, José Antonio. *Artículos inéditos de Unamuno en La Lucha de Clases, (1894–1897),* Bilbao: Ediciones Beta, 2002.

Evans, C. Stephen. "Apologetic Arguments in *Philosophical Fragments,*" Chap. 8 in *Kierkegaard on Faith and the Self.* Waco, TX: Baylor University Press, 2006, 133–49.

———. "Can God Be Hidden and Evident at the Same Time? Some Kierkegaardian Reflections," *Faith and Philosophy* 40.3 (2006): 241–53.

———. "Divine Commands: How Given and To Whom," Chap. 7 in *Kierkegaard's Ethic of Love: Divine Commands and Moral Requirements.* Oxford: Oxford University Press, 2004. 156–79.

———. "Is Kierkegaard an Irrationalist?" Chap. 7 in *Kierkegaard on Faith and the Self.* Waco, TX: Baylor University Press, 2006. 117–32.

———. *Kierkegaard: An Introduction.* Cambridge: Cambridge University Press, 2009.

———. "Truth and Subjectivity," Chap. 7 in *Kierkegaard's* Fragments *and* Postscript,: *The Religious Philosophy of Johannes Climacus.* Atlantic Highlands, N.J.: Humanities Press, 1983, 115–35.

Evans, Jan. *Unamuno and Kierkegaard: Paths to Selfhood in Fiction,* Lanham, MD: Lexington Books, 2005.

Bibliography

————. "Passion, Paradox and Indirect Communication: The Influence of *Postscript* on Miguel de Unamuno," in *Kierkegaard Studies Yearbook*, 2005, Eds. Niels Jørgen Cappelørn and Hermann Deuser. Berlin: Walter de Gruyter, 2005, 137–52.

Farré, Luis. *Unamuno, William James y Kierkegaard y otros ensayos*. Buenos Aires: Editorial La Aurora, 1967.

Fernández González, Angel-Raimundo. "Nueva lectura del *Diario íntimo* de Unamuno." *Cuadernos de la Cátedra Miguel de Unamuno* 32 (1997): 369–77.

Forero Ucros, Clemencia. "El deseo de inmortalidad en don Miguel de Unamuno." *Boletín Cultural y Bibiliográfico-Bilioteca*. 13.1 (1970): 49–64.

Franz, Thomas R. "Niebla and the Varieties of Religious Experience." *La Chispa: Selected Proceedings: The Sixth Louisiana Conference on Hispanic Languages and Literatures*. New Orleans: Tulane University, 1985. 103–13.

————. "Parenthood, Authorship and Immortality in Unamuno's Narratives." *Hispania* 63 (1980): 647–57.

Gelabert, Martín. "Dios, exigencia y pregunta del hombre según Unamuno." *Razón y fe* 213 (1986): 159–70.

Gómez, Michael. "Unamuno, Nietzsche and Religious Modernism: Affinities and Complexities Concerning the View of Faith." *Anales de la Literatura Española Contemporánea*. 35.1 2010): 223–54.

González Caminero, Nemesio. "Las dos etapas católicas de Unamuno." *Razón y fe*. 116 (Sept.-Oct., 1952): 210–39.

Hofkamp, Daniel. "Salamanca acoge a escritores evangélicos con los brazos abiertos." *Protestante Digital*. April 22, 2012. No pages. Online: http://www.protestantedigital. com/ES/Cultura/articulo/14408

James, William. *The Varieties of Religious Experience: A Study in Human Nature*. Modern Library, 1929. Gifford Lectures; History ebook Project. ACLS Humanities E book.

————. "The Will to Believe." *The Will to believe and Other Essays in Popular Philosophy*. Cambridge, MA: Harvard University Press, 1979.

Juan-Navarro, Santiago. "La reflexión sobre la inmortalidad en la obra de Unamuno: Filosofía de la existencia, epistemología y pensamiento religioso." *Cuadernos de Aldeeu*. 14.1–2. (1998): 235–52.

Kierkegaard, Søren. *Afsluttende Uvidenskabelig Efterskrift*, vol. 7, *Samlede Værker*. Københaven: Drachmann, Heiberg og Lange, 1902

————. *The Concept of Anxiety*. Ed. and Trans. Reidar Thomte. Princeton: Princeton University Press, 1980.

————. *Concluding Unscientific Postscript to Philosophical Fragments*. Vol. 1. Ed. and Trans. Howard and Edna Hong. Princeton: Princeton University Press, 1992.

————. *Eighteen Upbuilding Discourses*. Ed. and Trans. Howard and Edna Hong. Princeton: Princeton University Press, 1990.

————. *Either/Or*. Vols. 1 & 2. Ed. and Trans. Howard and Edna Hong. Princeton: Princeton University Press, 1987.

————. *Fear and Trembling, Repetition*. Ed. and Trans. Howard and Edna Hong. Princeton: Princeton University Press, 1980.

————. *Philosophical Fragments* and *Johannes Climacus*. Ed. and Trans. Howard V. Hong and Edna H. Hong. Princeton: Princeton University Press, 1985.

————. *The Point of View of My Work as an Author*. Ed. and Trans. Howard and Edna Hong. Princeton: Princeton University Press, 1998.

————. *Purity of Heart is to Will One Thing.* Trans. Douglas V. Steers. New York: Harper, 1956.

————. *Søren Kierkegaard's Journals and Papers.* Ed. and Trans. Howard V. Hong and Edna H. Hong, assisted by Gregor Malantschuk. Bloomington: Indiana University Press, (Vol. 1) 1967, (Vol. 2) 1970, (Vols. 3–4) 1975, (Vols. 5–7) 1978.

————. *The Sickness Unto Death.* Ed. and Trans. Howard and Edna Hong. Princeton: Princeton University Press, 1980.

————. *Upbuilding Discourses in Various Spirits.* Ed. and Trans. Howard and Edna Hong. Princeton: Princeton University Press, 1993.

————. *Works of Love.* Ed. and Trans. Howard V. Hong and Edna H. Hong. Princeton: Princeton University Press, 1995.

Kreeft, Peter. *Christianity for Modern Pagans: Pascal's Pensees.* San Francisco: Ignatius Press, 1993.

Lapuente, Felipe. "Unamuno y la Iglesia Católica: Reacción crítica," in *Actas del X Congreso de la Asociación Internacional de Hispanistas, Barcelona, 21–26 de agosto de 1989,* Barcelona: PPU, 1992. 25–33.

Levi, Albert. "The Quixotic Quest for Being," *Ethics* 66 (January 1956): 132–36.

Malvido Miguel, Eduardo. *Unamuno a la busca de la inmortalidad.* Salamanca: Ediciones San Pio X, 1977.

Marías, Julián. *Miguel de Unamuno.* Barcelona: Gustavo Gili, 1968.

Nozick, Martin. *Miguel de Unamuno: The Agony of Belief.* Princeton: Princeton University Press, 1971.

Orringer, Nelson. *Unamuno y los protestantes liberales* (1912). Madrid: Gredos, 1985.

————. "'Translator's Introduction'" to *Treatise on Love of God,* by M. de Unamuno, Urbana and Chicago: University of Illinois Press, 2007. xi–xxxviii.

Ouimette, Victor. *Reason Aflame.* New Haven: Yale University Press, 1974.

Pascal, Blaise. *Pascal Pensées.* Trans. A. J. Krailsheimer. Middlesex, England and Baltimore, MD: Penguin Books, 1966.

Poole, Roger. *Kierkegaard: The Indirect Communication.* Charlottesville: University Press of Virginia, 1993.

Sánchez Barbudo, Antonio. *Estudios sobre Unamuno y Machado.* Madrid: Guadarrama, 1968.

————. "La formación del pensamiento de Unamuno. Una experiencia decisiva: la crisis de 1897." *Hispanic Review.* 18.3 (July, 1950): 95–122.

Unamuno, Miguel de. *De patriotismo espiritual. Artículos en La nación de Buenos Aires,* 1901–1914. Ed. Víctor Ouimette, Salamanca: Ediciones Universidad de Salamanca, 1997.

————. *Obras completas.* Ed. M. García Blanco. 9 Vols. Madrid: Escelicer, 1966–71.

————. *Abel Sánchez.* 1917. *Obras completas,* 1967. 2: 683–759.

————. *La agonía del cristianismo.* 1926. *Obras completas,* 1967. 7:307–64.

————. *El Cristo de Velázquez.* 1920. *Obras completas.* 1969. 6:417–93.

————. *Del sentimiento trágico de la vida en los hombres y en los pueblos.* 1913. *Obras completas,* 1967. 7: 106–302.

————. *Diario íntimo.* 1897–1902. *Obras completas,* 1966. 8: 773–880.

————. *En torno al casticismo.* 1895. *Obras completas,* 1966. 1: 775–856.

————. "Espíritu de la raza vasca." 1887. *Obras completas,* 1968. 4: 153–74.

————. "La fe." 1903. *Obras completas.* 1966. 1: 962–971.

————. "Ibsen y Kierkegaard." 1907. *Obras completas,* 1968. 3: 289–93.

Bibliography

————. "Mi religion." 1907. *Obras completas,* 1968. 3: 259–63.

————. Paz en la guerra. 1897. Obras completas. 1967. 2: 87–301.

————. "¿Qué es verdad?" 1906. Obras completas. 1968. 3:854–64.

————. Recuerdos de niñez y de mocedad. 1908. Obras completas. 1967, 8: 95–175.

————. *San Manuel Bueno, mártir.* 1930. *Obras completas,* 1967. 2: 1113–54.

————. "Soledad." 1905 *Obras completas,* 1966. 1:1251–63

————. *La venda.* 1912 *Obras completas,* 1968. 5: 221–44.

————. *Vida de Don Quijote y Sancho.* 1904. *Obras completas,* 1968. 3:49–254.

————. *Tratado del amor de Dios.* Ed. Nelson Orringer. Madrid: Editorial Tecnos, 2005.

Urrutia León, Manuel María. *Miguel de Unamuno desconocido con 58 nuevos textos de Unamuno,* Salamanca: Ediciones Universidad, 2007.

Walsh, Sylvia. *Living Poetically: Kierkegaard's Existential Aesthetics.* University Park: Pennsylvania State University Press, 1994.

Zubizarreta, Armando F. *Unamuno y su "nívola".* Madrid: Taurus, 1960.

Index